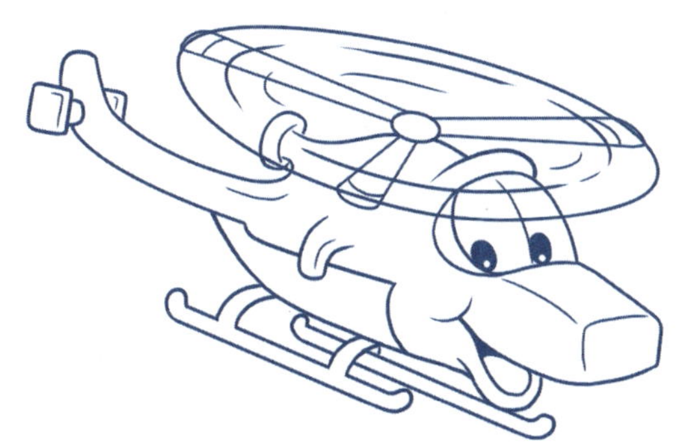

My name is

....

Are you ready to write?

Posture

Is your back resting against the chair?

Are your feet flat on the floor?

Paper position

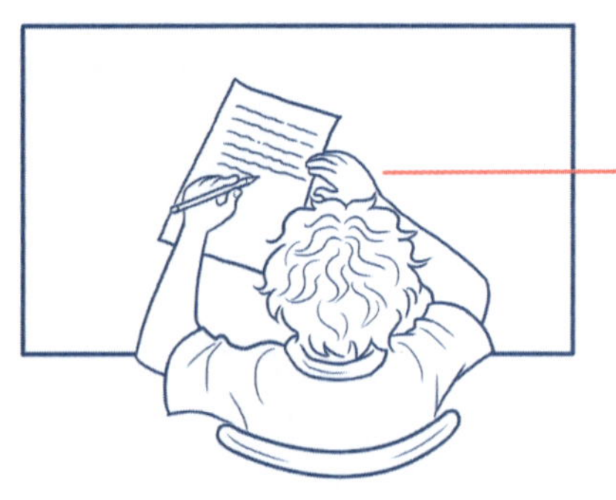

left-handed

Are you holding the paper steady with your non-writing hand?

right-handed

Pencil grip

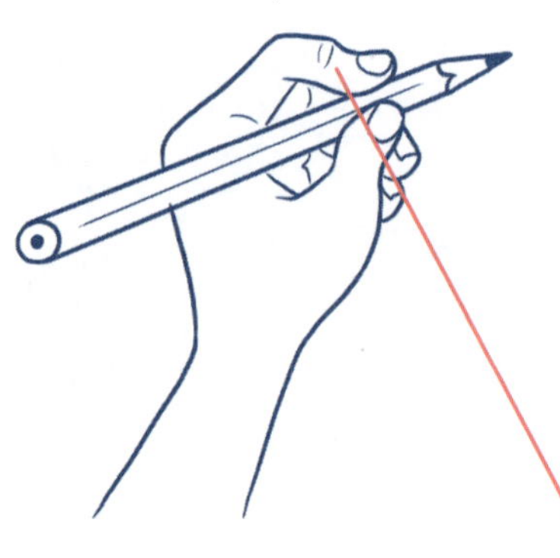

Is one finger on top of the pencil?

Left-handers, hold your pencil a little higher so you can see your handwriting!

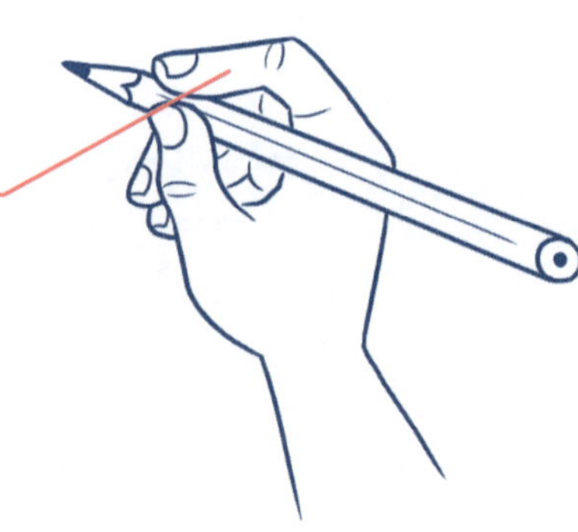

Start at the red dots. Follow the arrows.

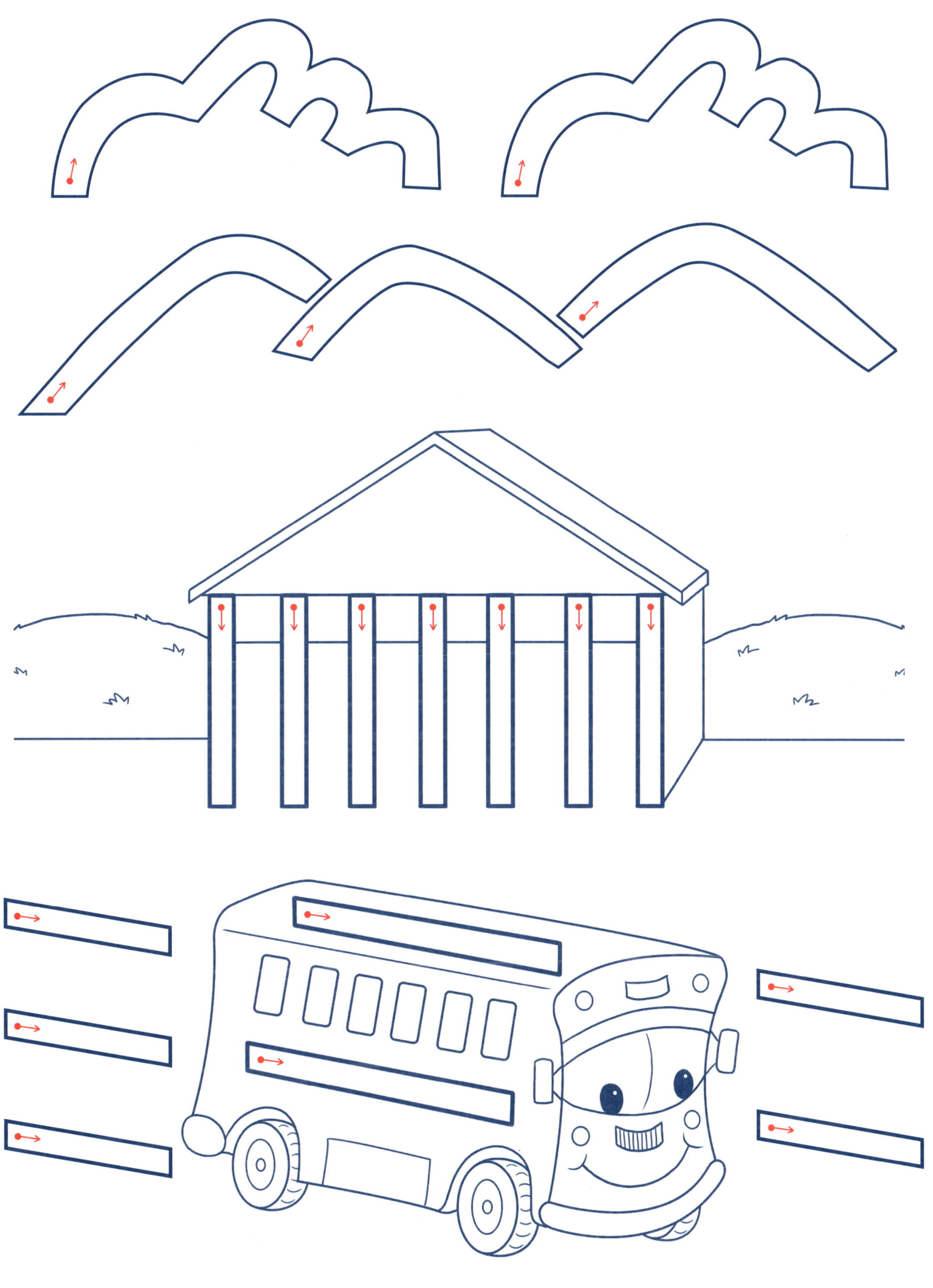

Start at the red dots. Follow the arrows.

Start at the red dots. Follow the arrows.

Start at the red dots. Follow the arrows.

Start at the red dots. Follow the arrows.

Start at the red dots. Follow the arrows.

r is a body letter.

Trace all the body letters.

a c e i m n o r

s u v w x z

b is a head and body letter.

Trace all the head and body letters.

b d f h k l t

g is a body and tail letter.

Trace all the body and tail letters.

g j p q y

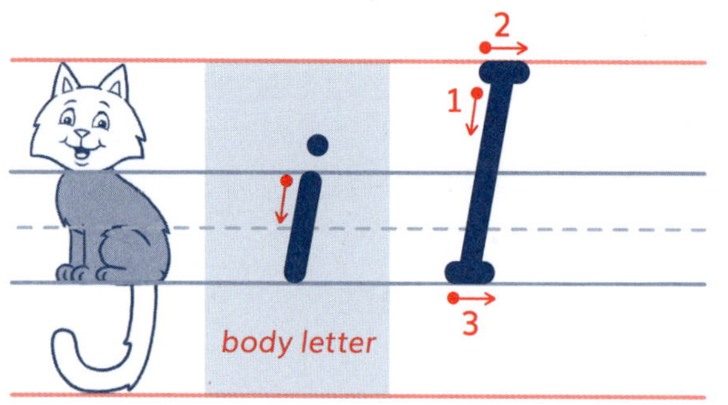

ice cream

Start at the red dot. Follow the arrow.

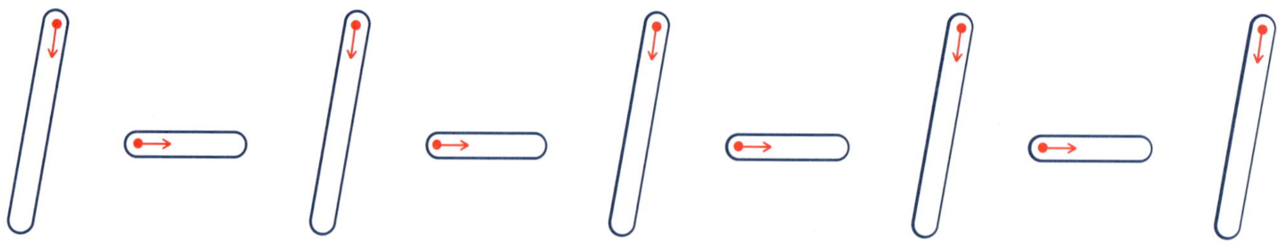

Track.

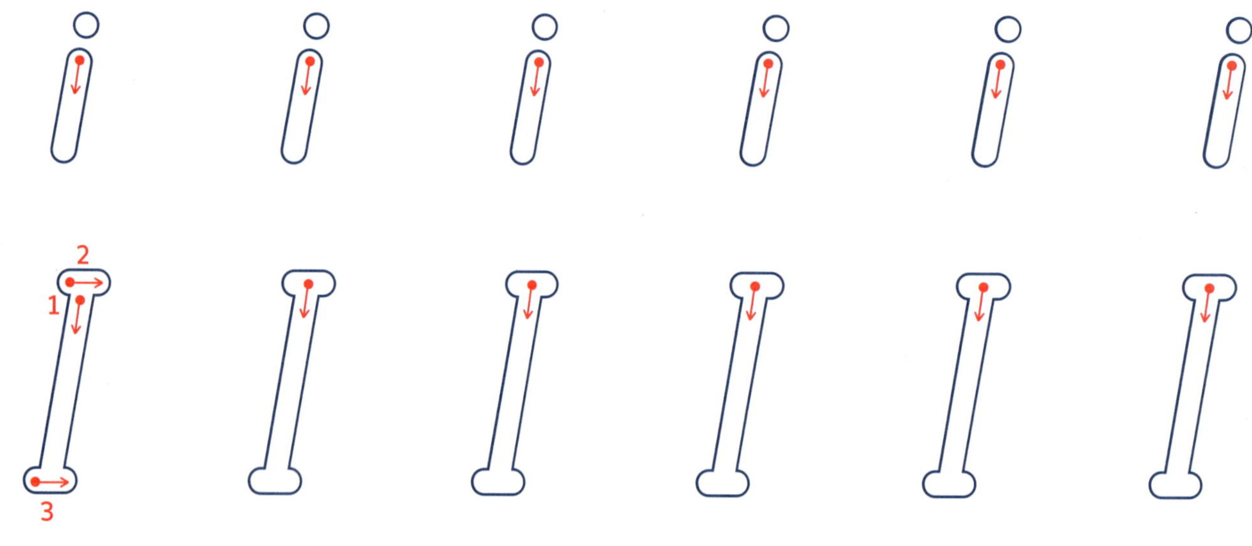

Find **i**.

Trace and copy.

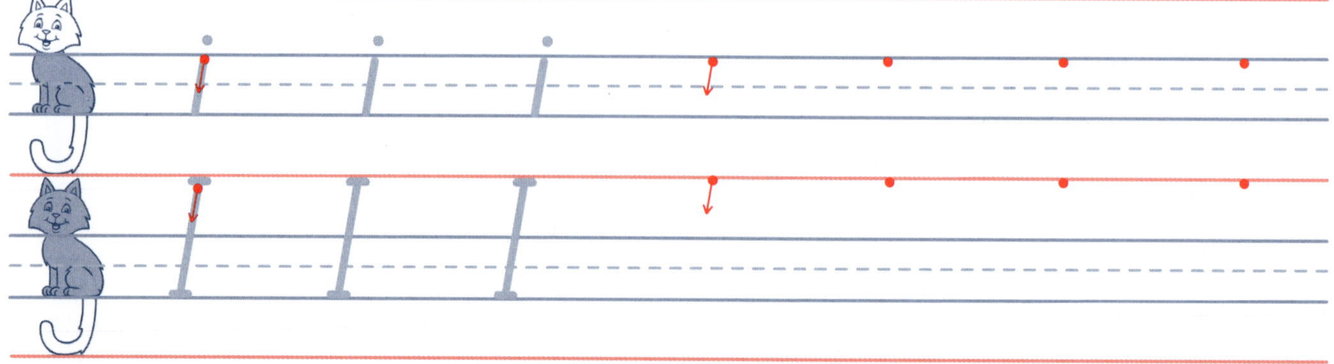

Trace and copy.

inside inside inside

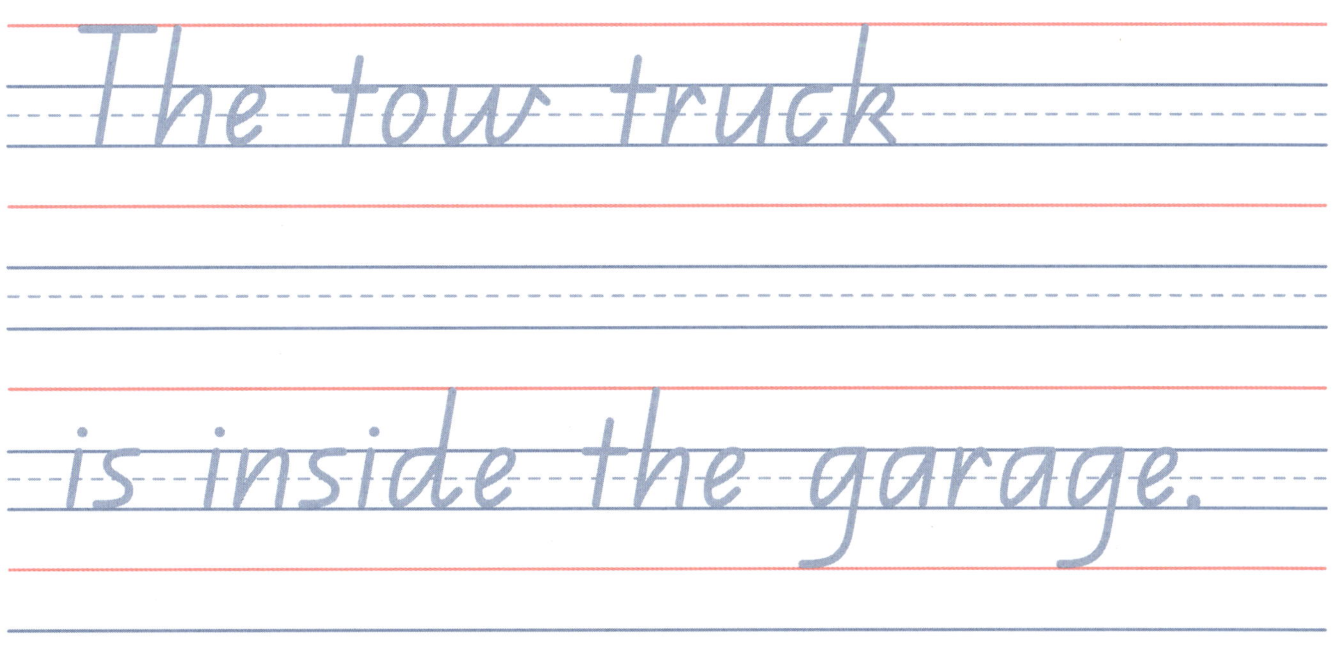

Trace and copy.

The tow truck

is inside the garage.

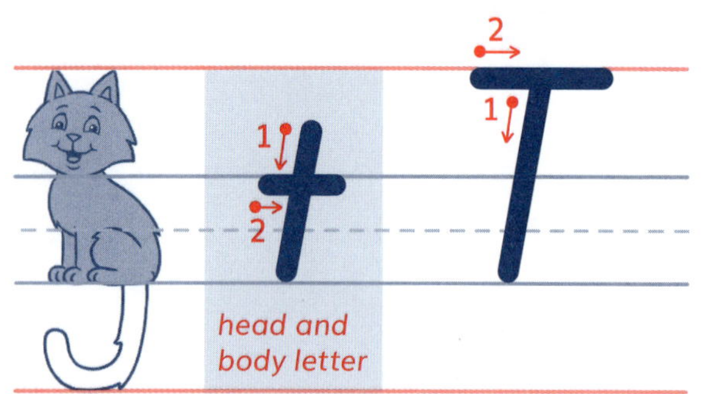

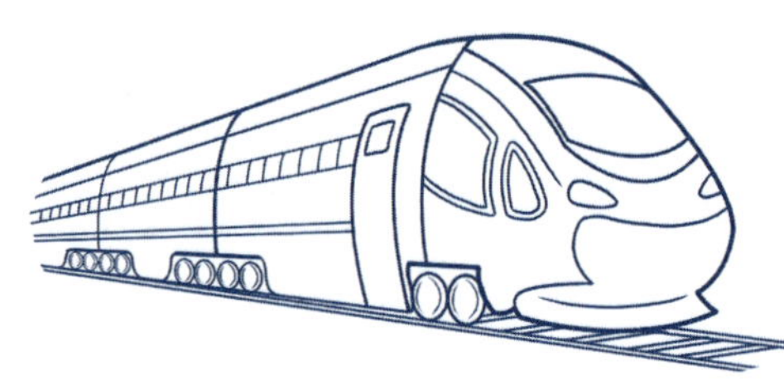

train

Start at the red dot. Follow the arrow.

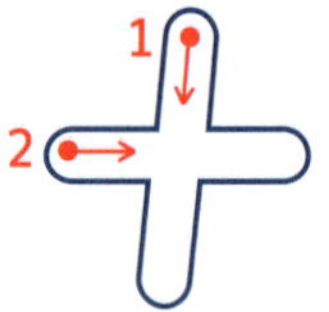
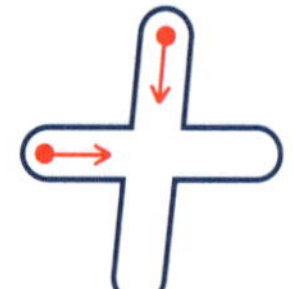
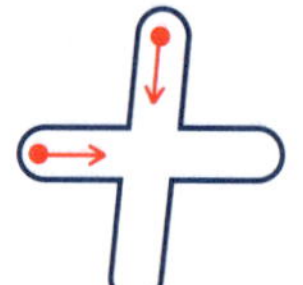
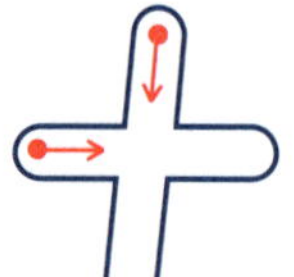
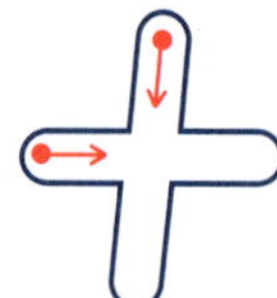

Track.

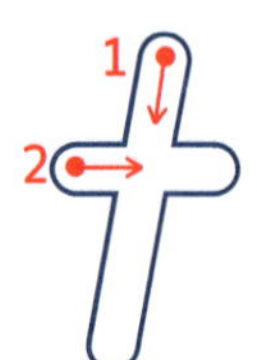

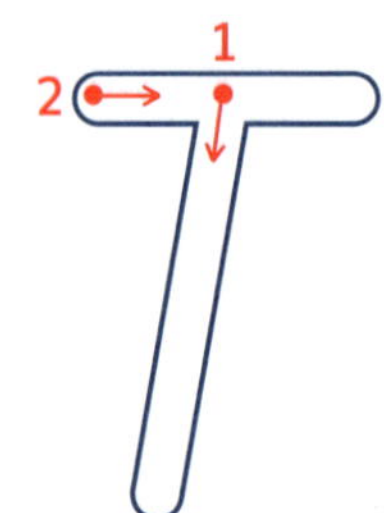
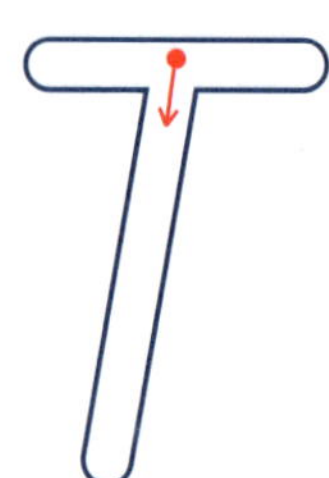
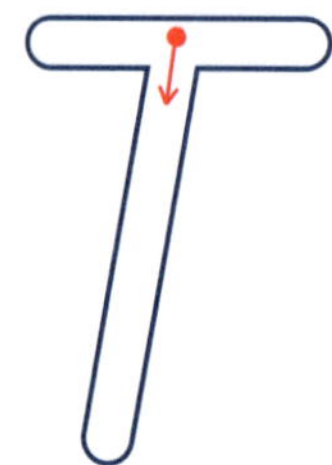
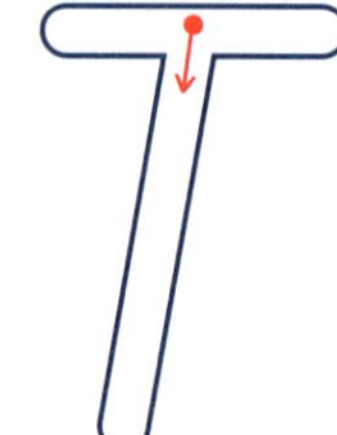
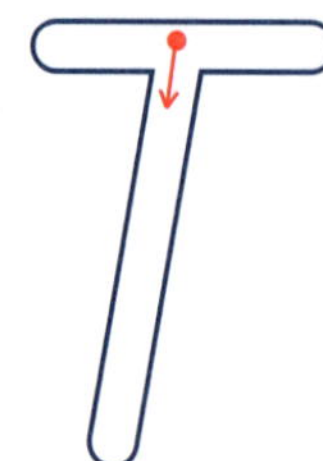

Find **t**.

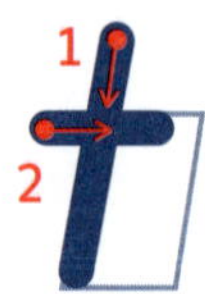
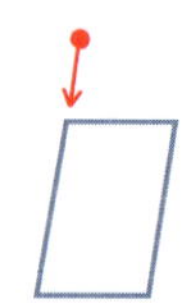
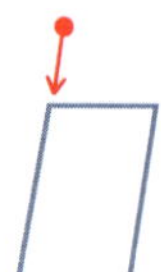
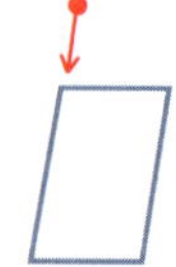
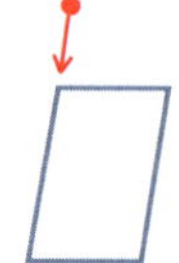
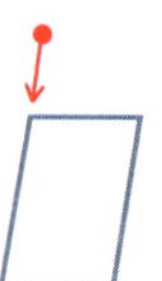

Trace and copy.

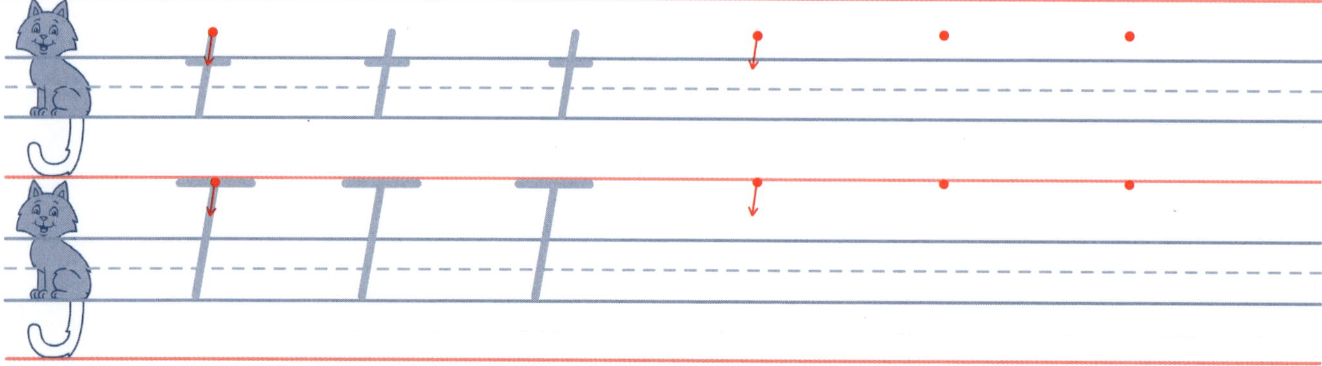

Trace and copy.

Trace and copy.

Toytown tow truck

needs a new tyre.

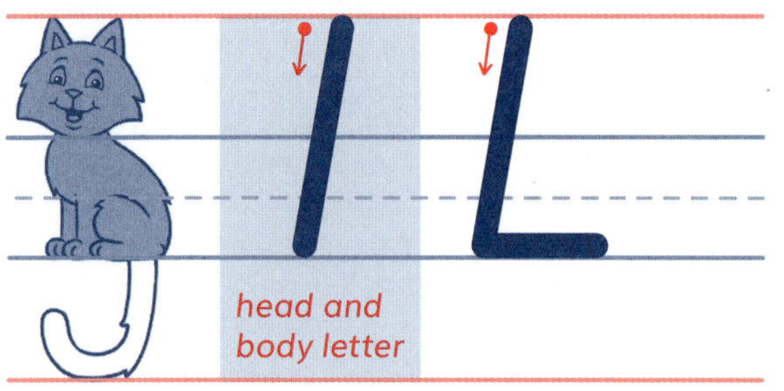

legs

Start at the red dot. Follow the arrow.

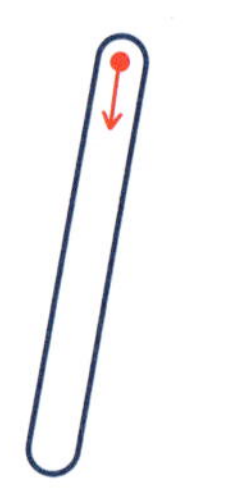 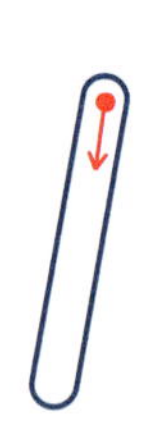 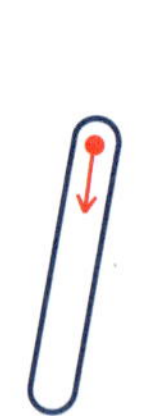  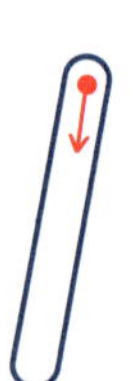 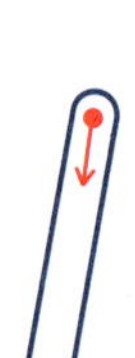  

Track.

  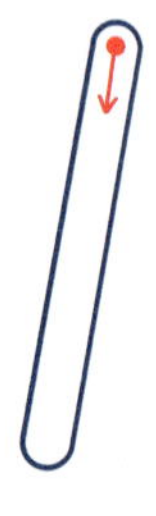  

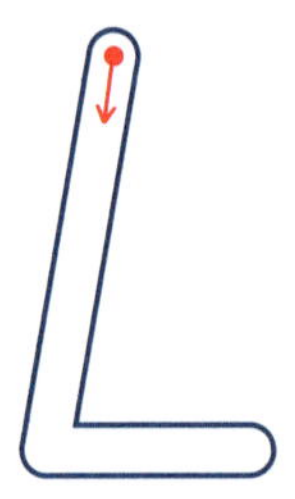 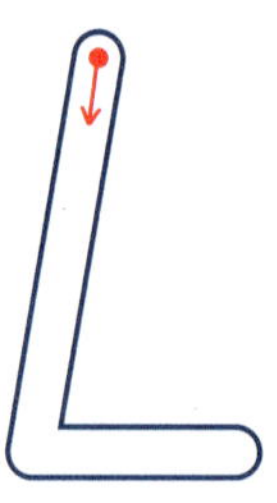 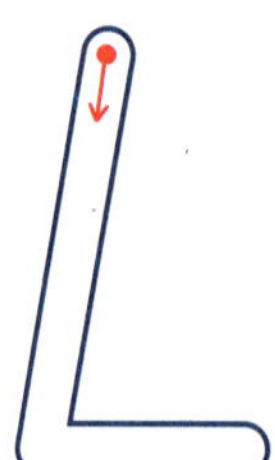 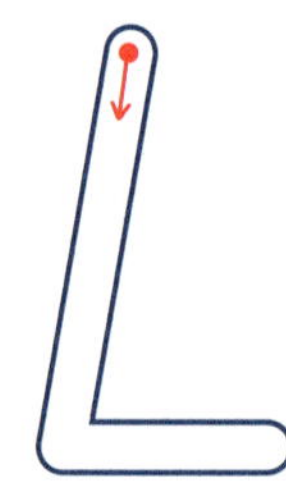 

Find **l**.

 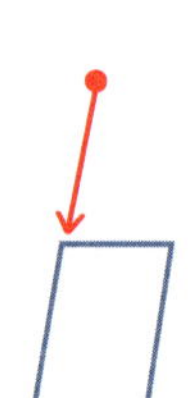 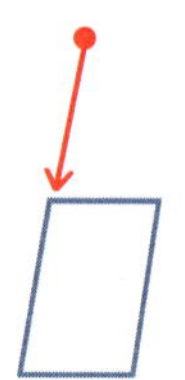 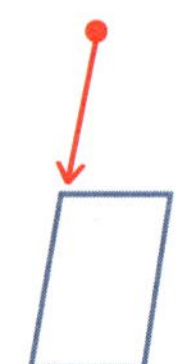 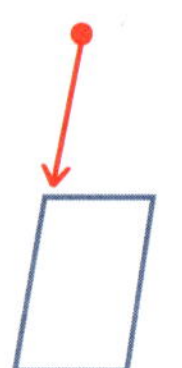

Trace and copy.

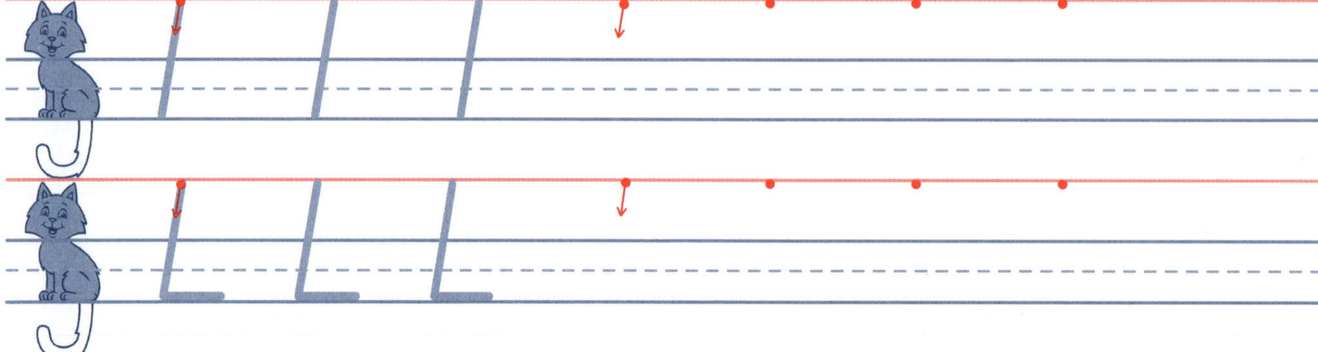

Trace and copy.

looks looks looks

Trace and copy.

The Toytown bus

looks at the flat tyre.

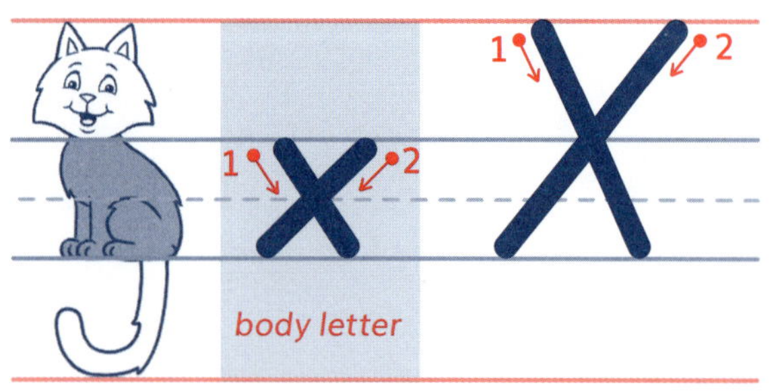

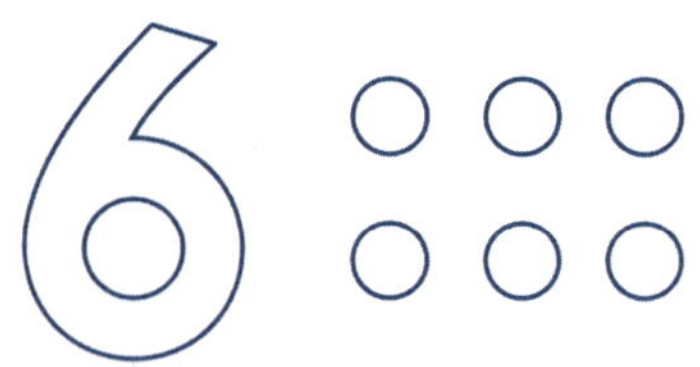

Start at the red dot. Follow the arrow.

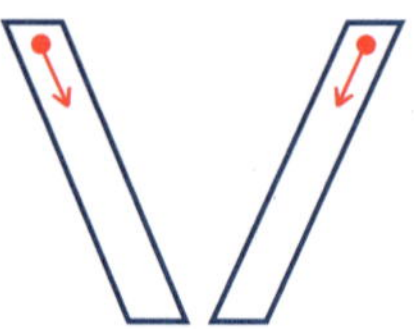 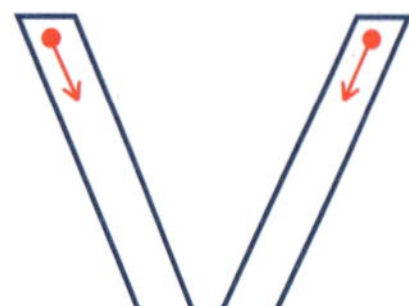 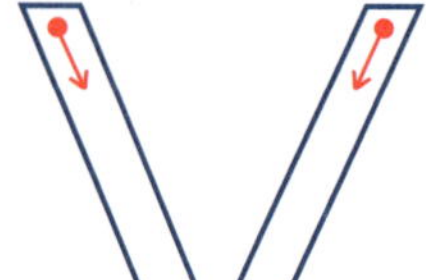 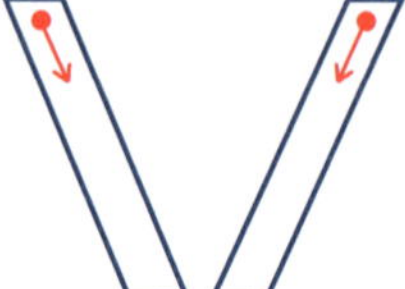

Track.

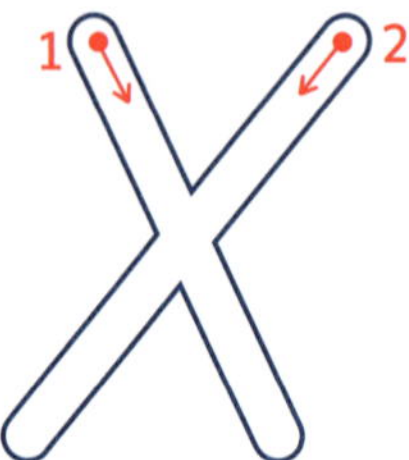

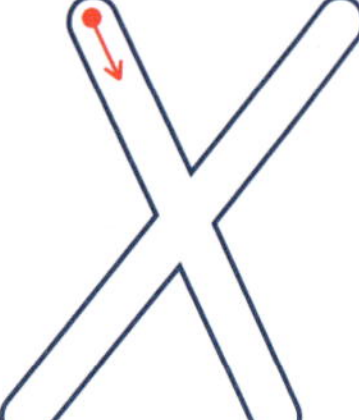 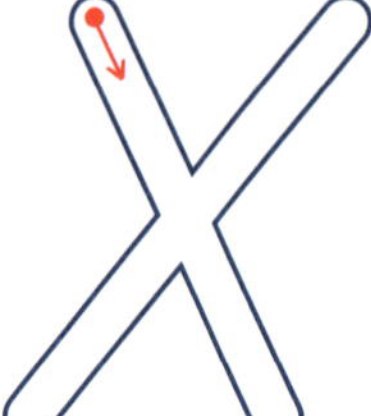 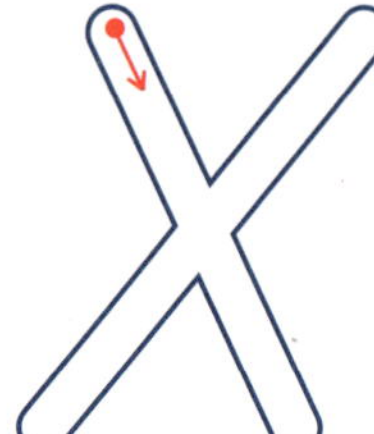 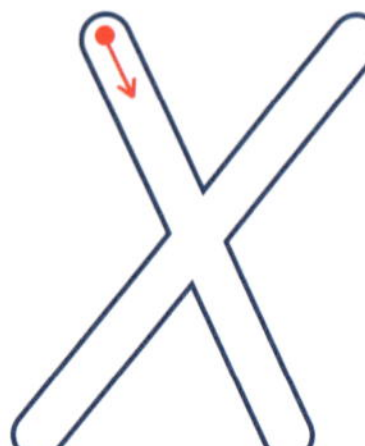

Find **x**.

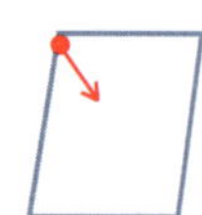 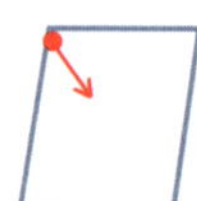 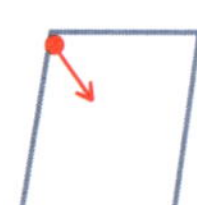 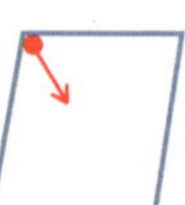

Trace and copy.

Trace and copy.

fix fix fix fix

Trace and copy.

"I will fix your tyre,"

says the Toytown bus.

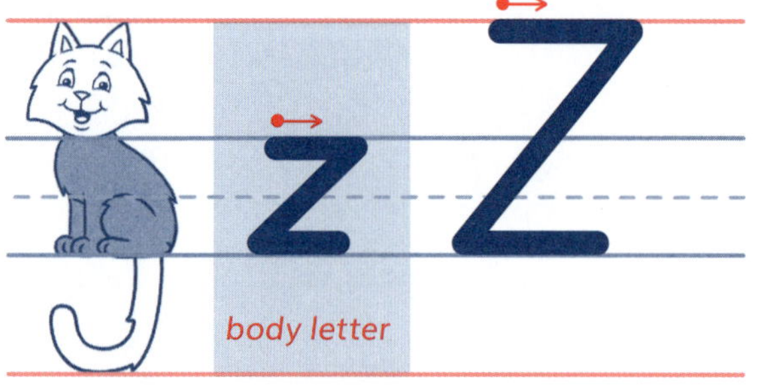

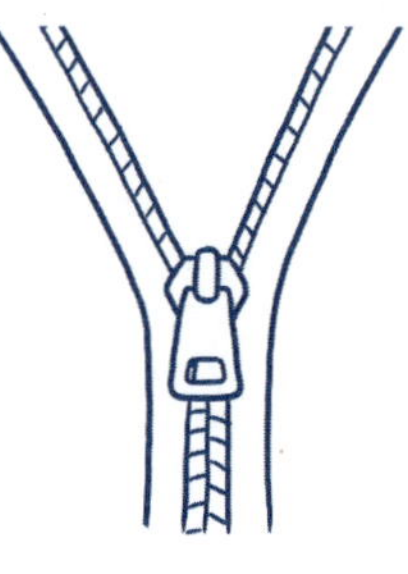

zip

Start at the red dot. Follow the arrow.

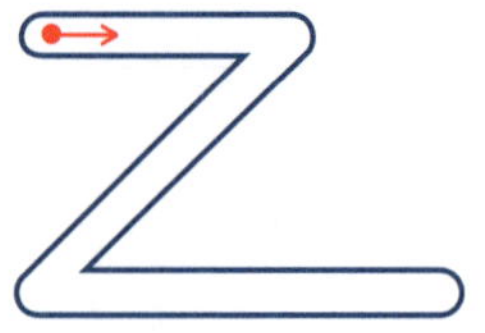 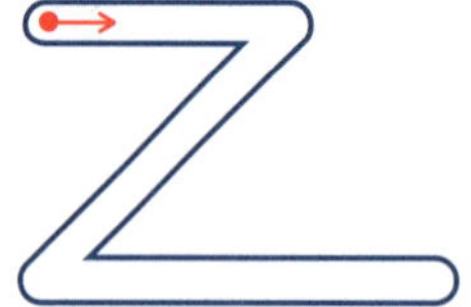 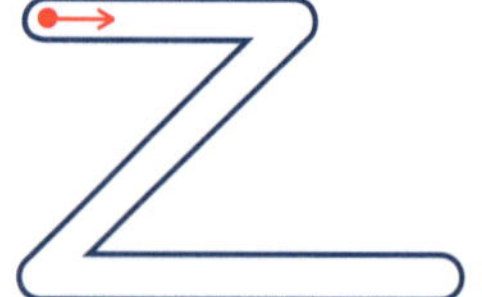 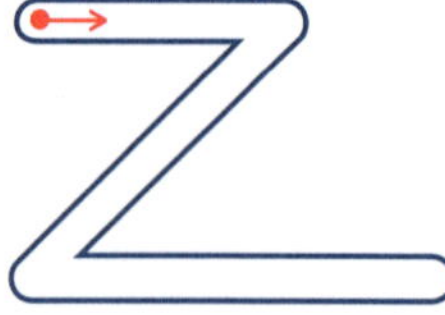

Track.

Find **z**.

 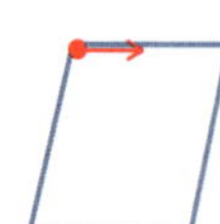 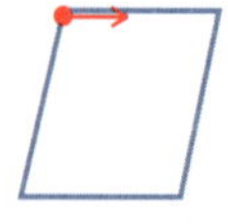 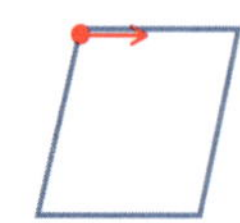 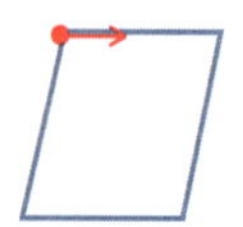

Trace and copy.

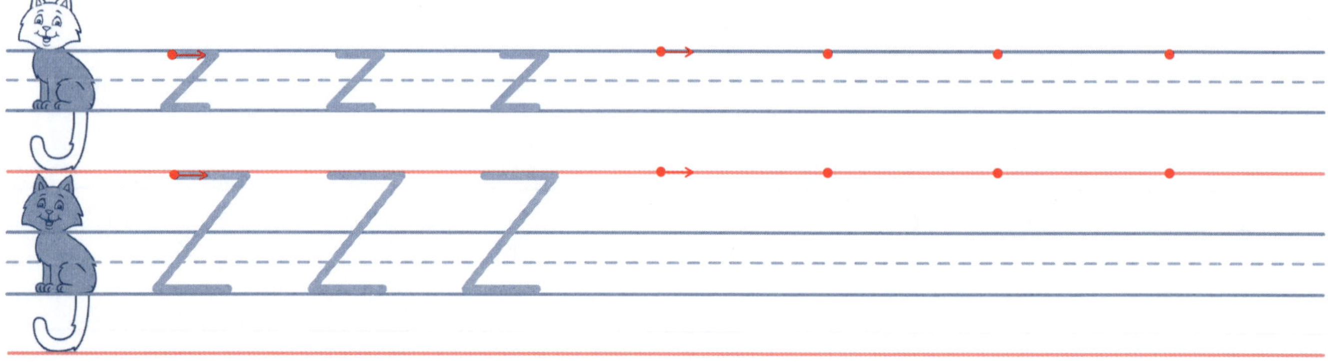

Trace and copy.

zoom zoom zoom

get.ga/PMWA8

Trace and copy.

The tow truck can

zoom away now.

Start at the red dot. Follow the arrow.

Track.

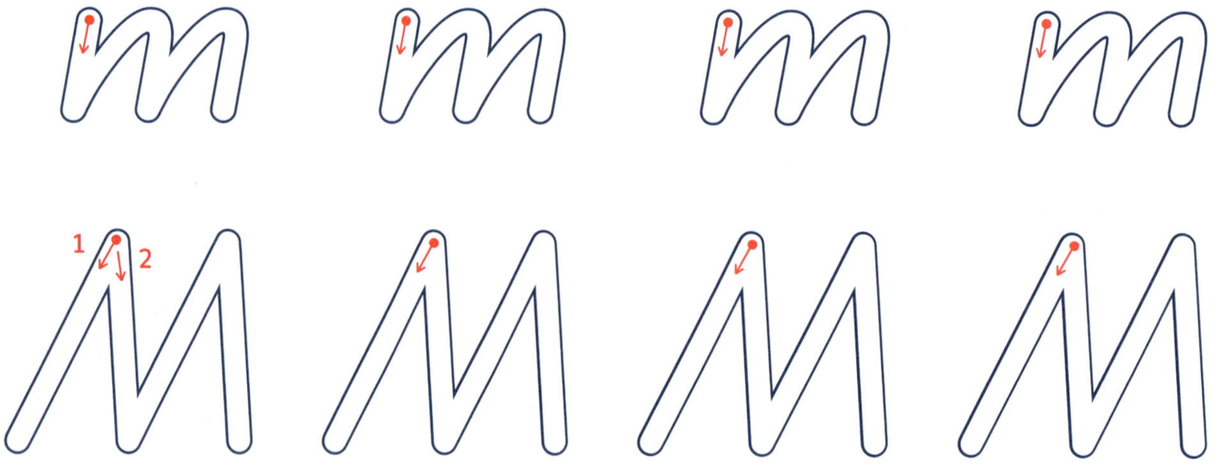

Find **m** and colour the wedges.

Trace and copy.

Trace and copy.

mountain mountain

Trace and copy.

Toytown helicopter

went over the mountain.

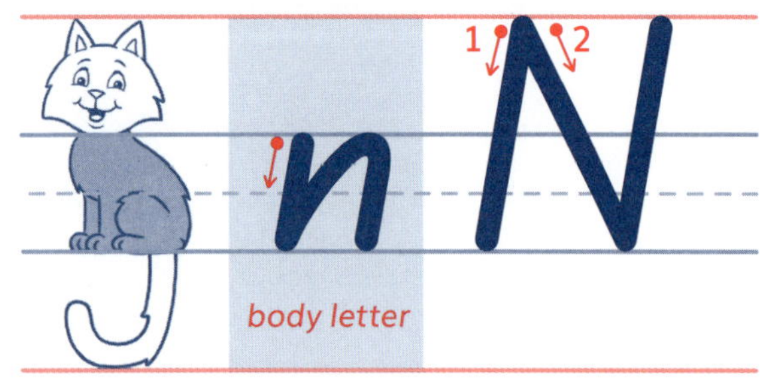

nuts

Start at the red dot. Follow the arrow.

Track.

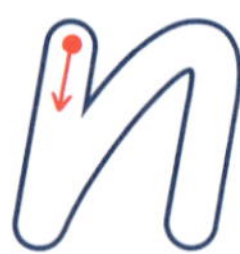    

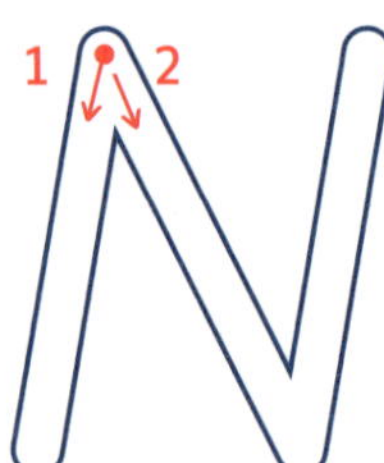 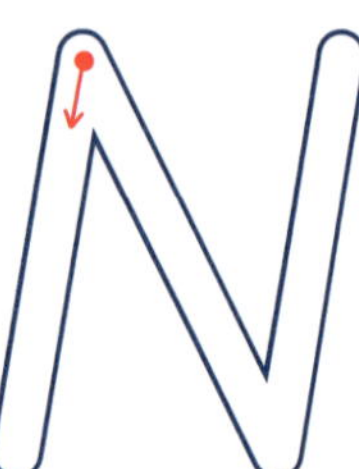 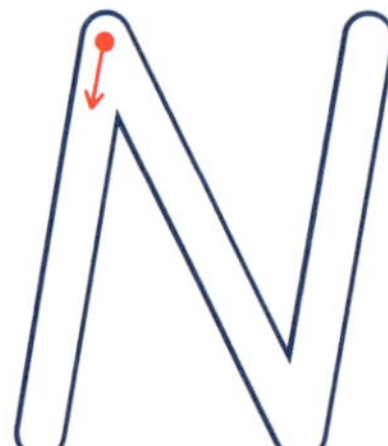  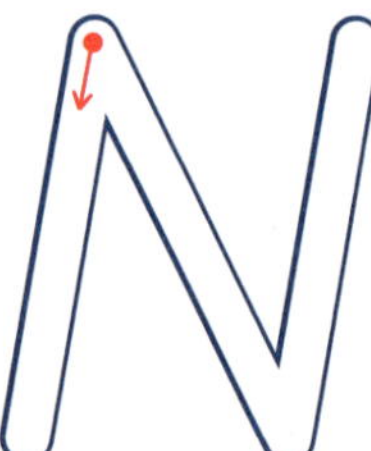

Find **n** and colour the wedge.

 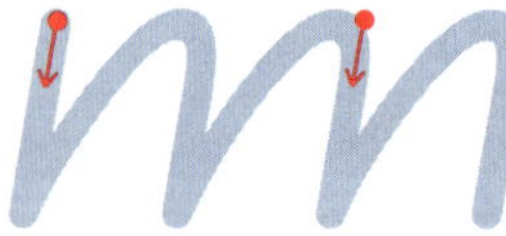 

Trace and copy.

Trace and copy.

not not not not

Trace and copy.

The scared little cat

could not get down.

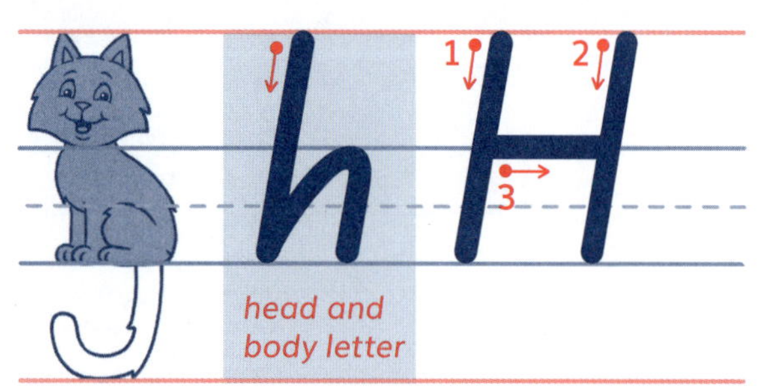

helicopter

Start at the red dot. Follow the arrow.

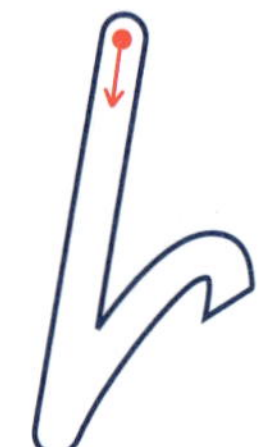    

Track.

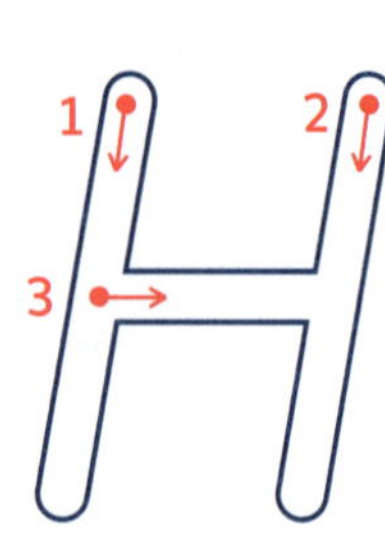

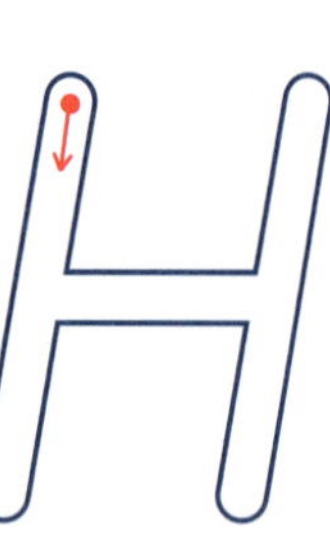 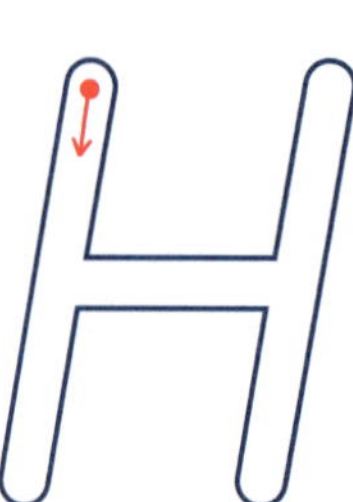 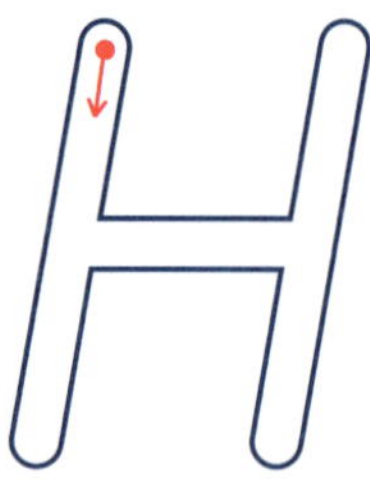 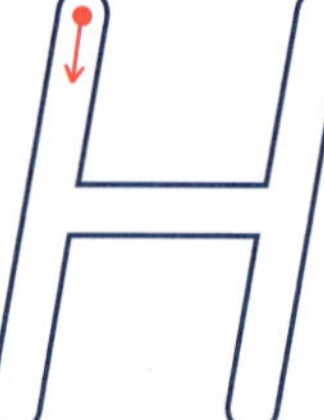

Find **h** and colour the wedge.

 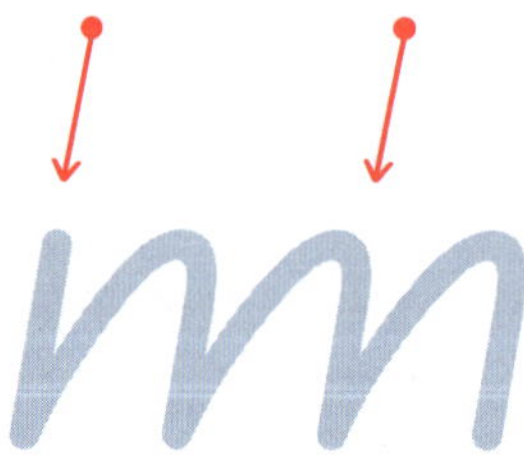 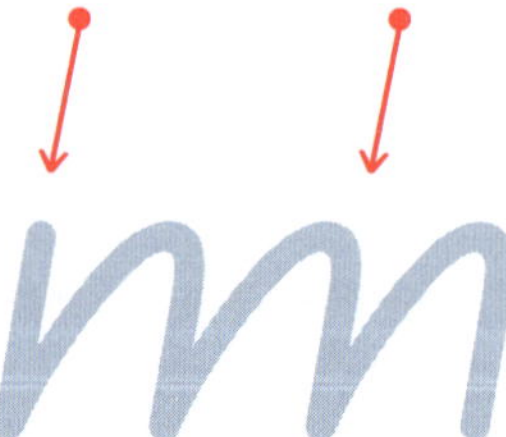

Trace and copy.

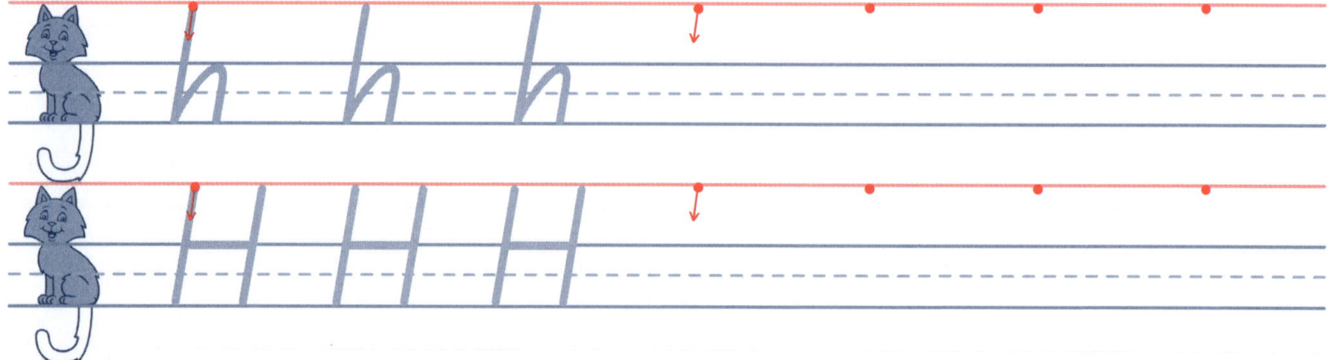

Trace and copy.

help help help help

Trace and copy.

"Hurry, fire engine.

We need your help."

Start at the red dot. Follow the arrow.

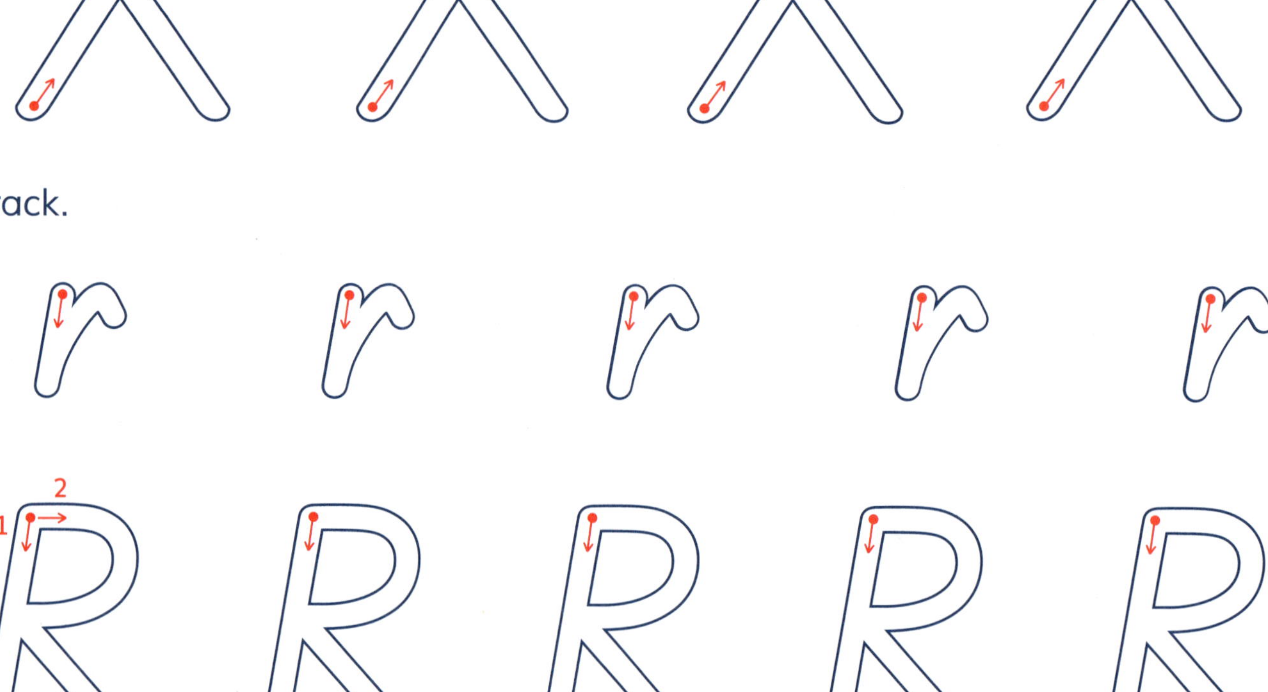

Track.

Find **r** and colour the wedge.

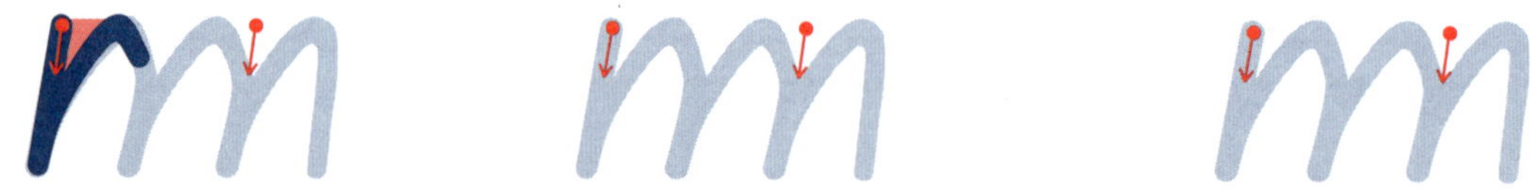

Trace and copy.

Trace and copy.

roof roof roof roof

get.ga/PMWA9

Trace and copy.

"There is a little cat

here on the roof."

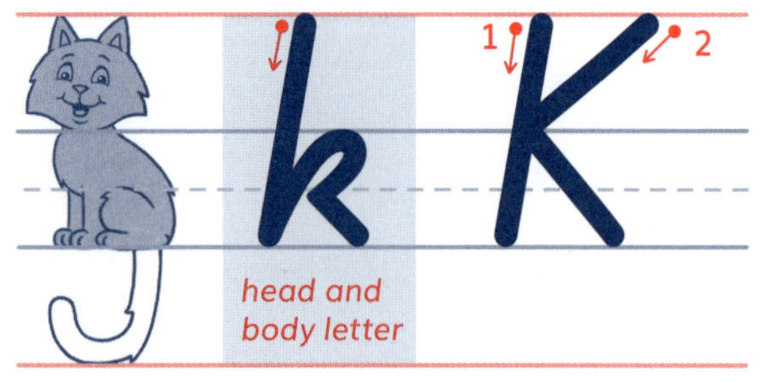

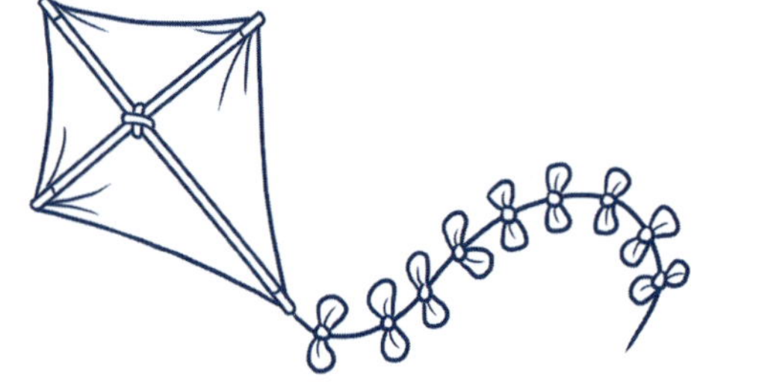

kite

Start at the red dot. Follow the arrow.

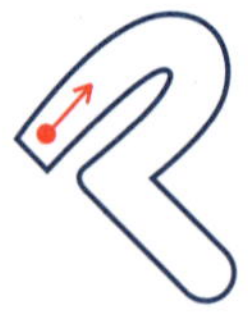 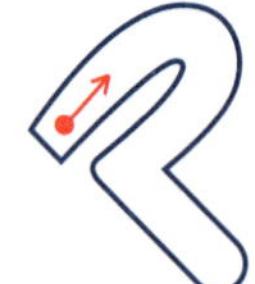 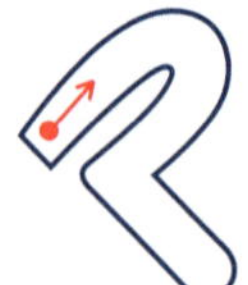  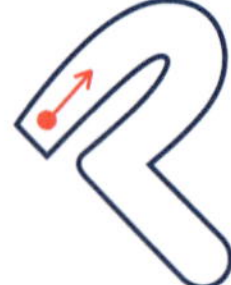

Track.

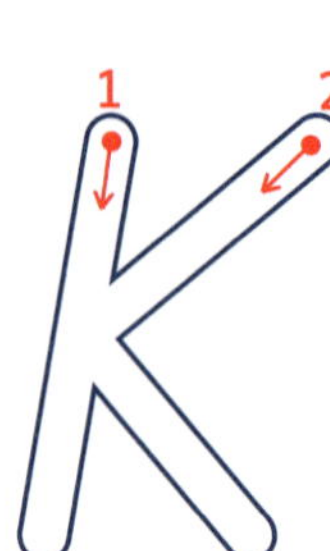

  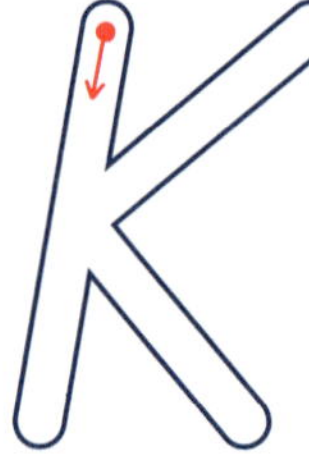 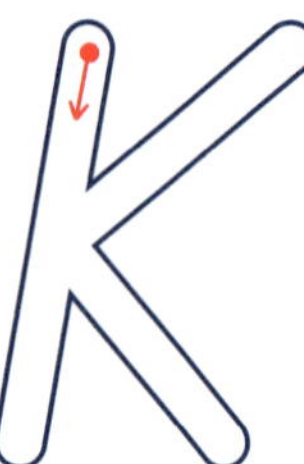

Find **k** and colour the wedge.

 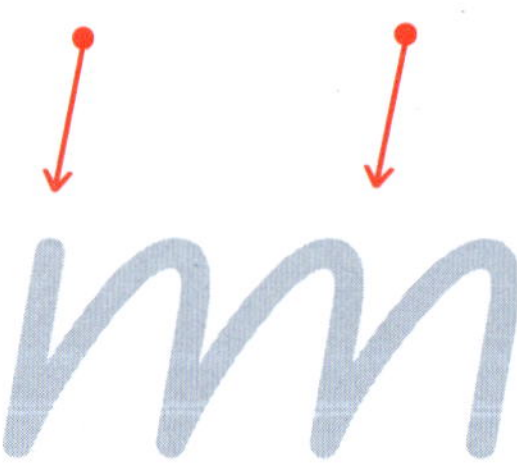 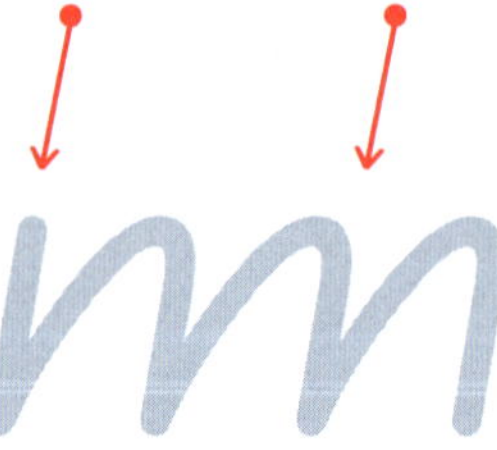

Trace and copy.

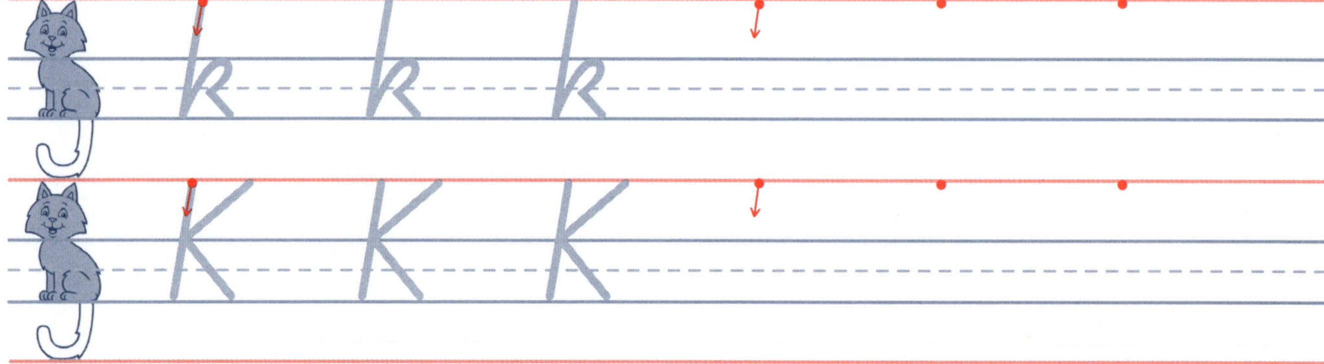

Trace and copy.

keep keep keep keep

Trace and copy.

"Little cat, keep still.

I will help you."

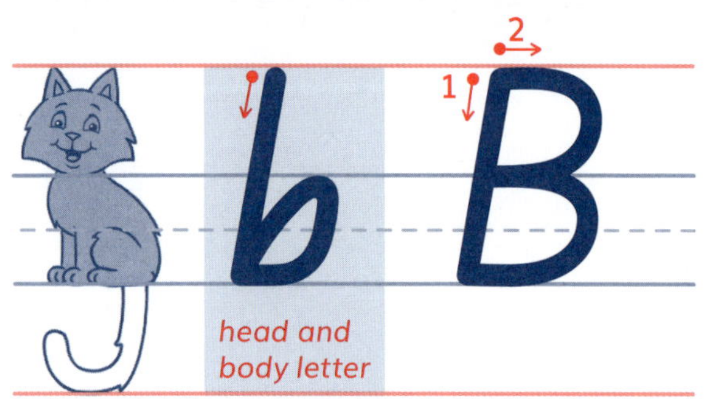

bear

Start at the red dot. Follow the arrow.

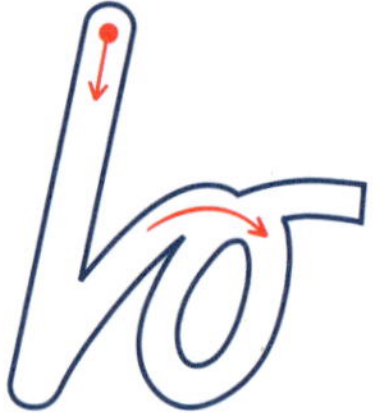 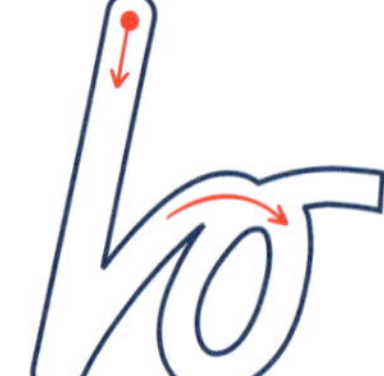 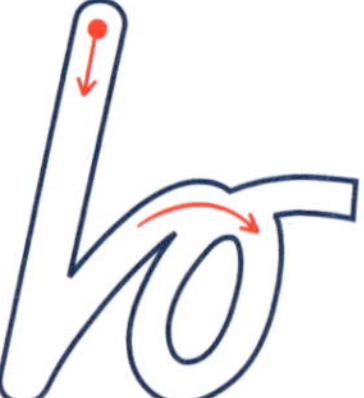 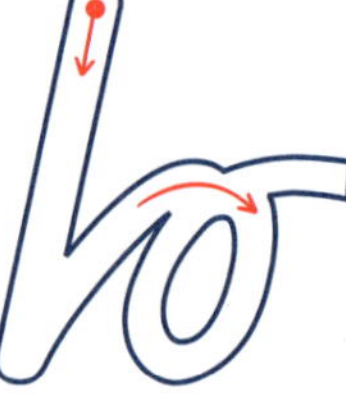

Track.

Find **b** and colour the wedge.

 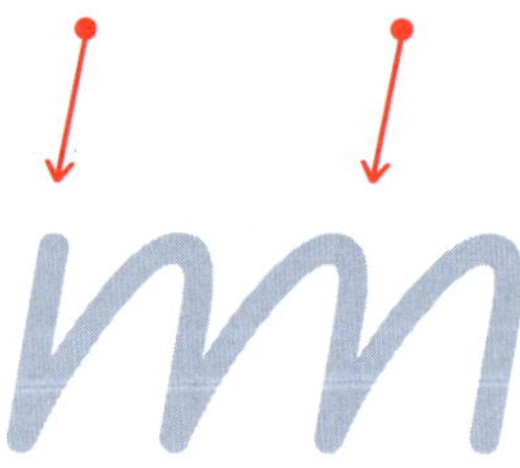 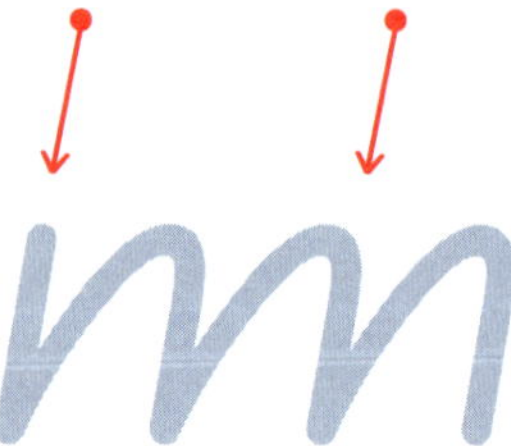

Trace and copy.

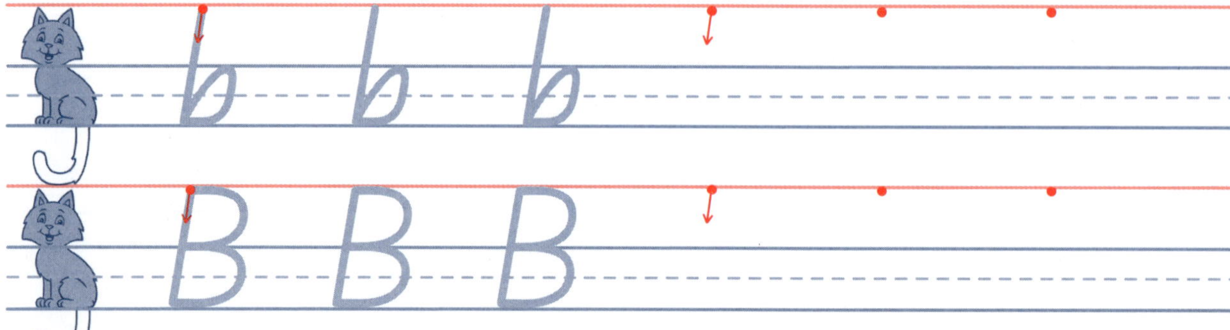

Trace and copy.

beside beside beside

Trace and copy.

Fire engine stopped

beside the house.

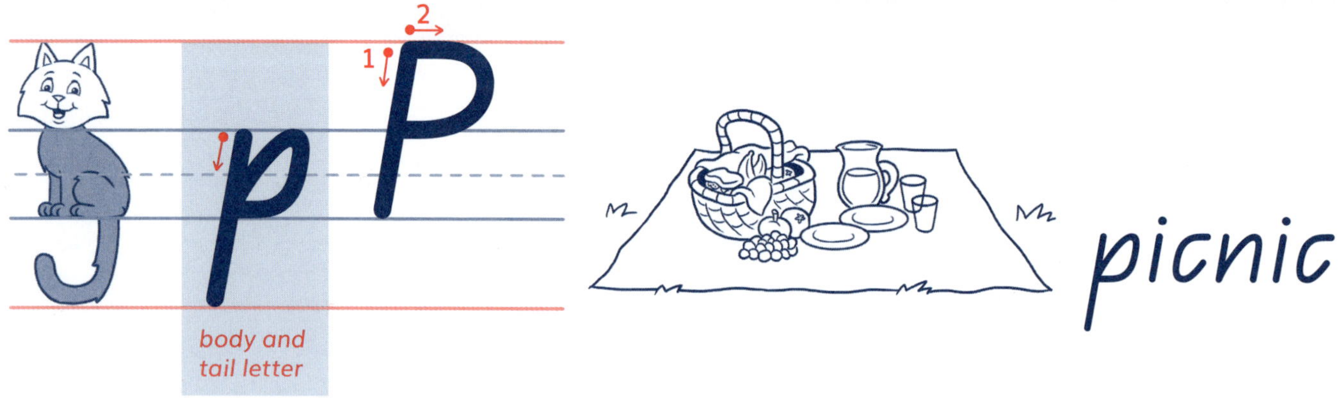

Start at the red dot. Follow the arrow.

Track.

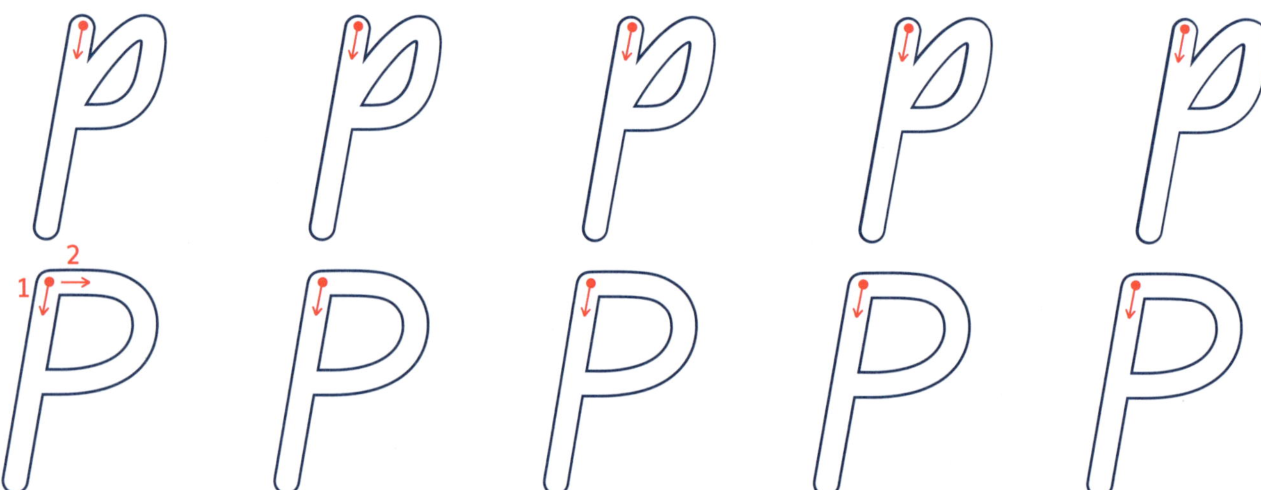

Find **p** and colour the wedge.

Trace and copy.

Trace and copy.

Trace and copy.

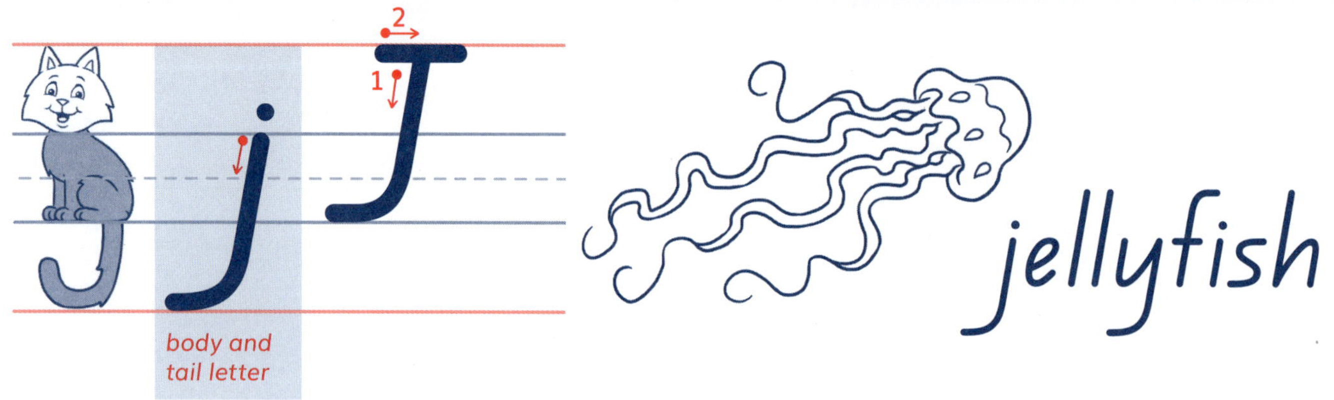

Start at the red dot. Follow the arrow.

Track.

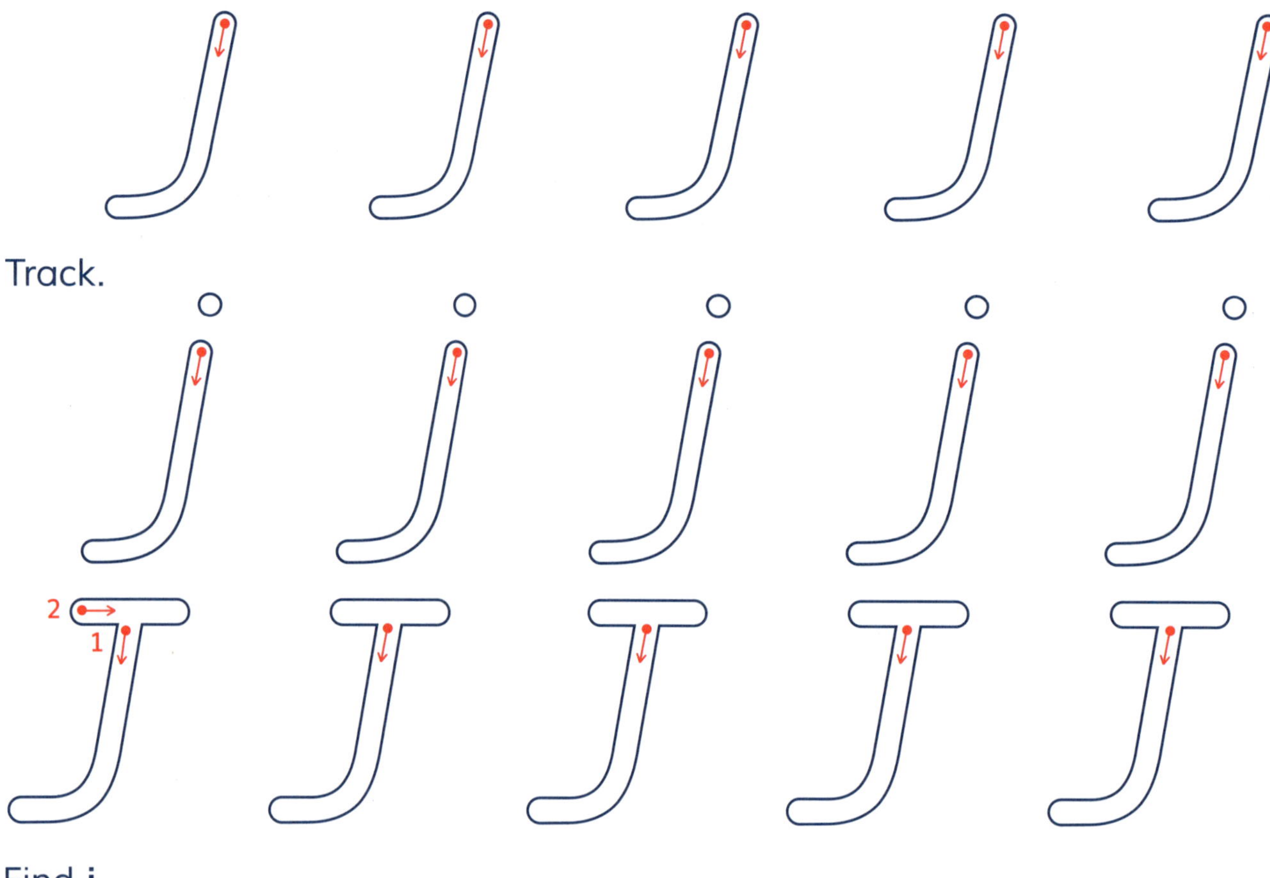

Find **j**.

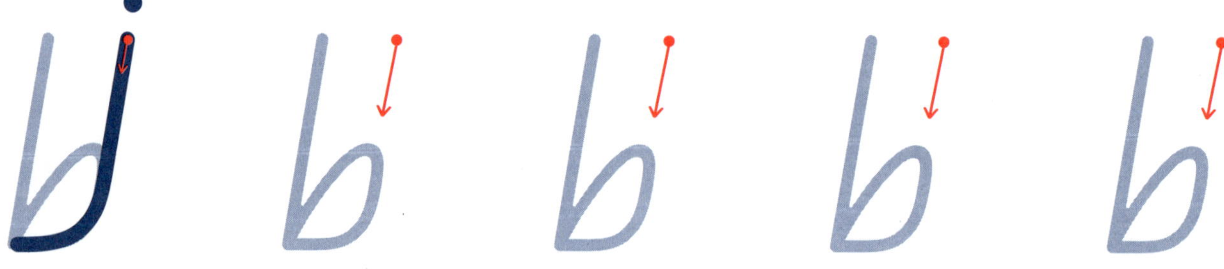

Trace and copy.

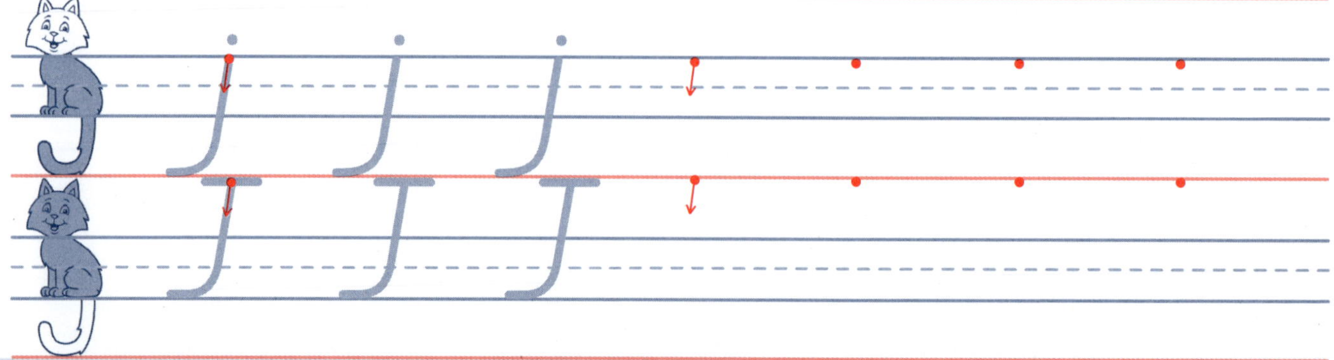

Trace and copy.

get.ga/PMWA10

Trace and copy.

said the helicopter.

Start at the red dot. Follow the arrow.

Track.

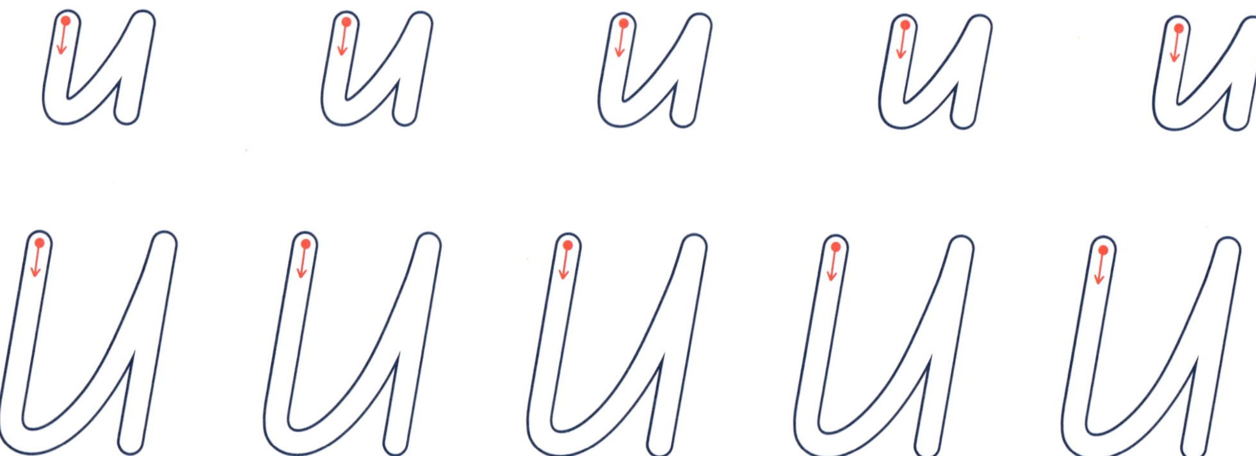

Find **u** and colour the wedge.

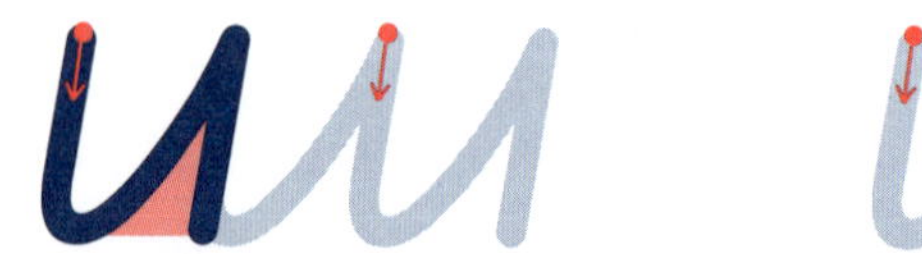

Trace and copy.

Trace and copy.

up up up up

Trace and copy.

The Toytown bus

went up the hill.

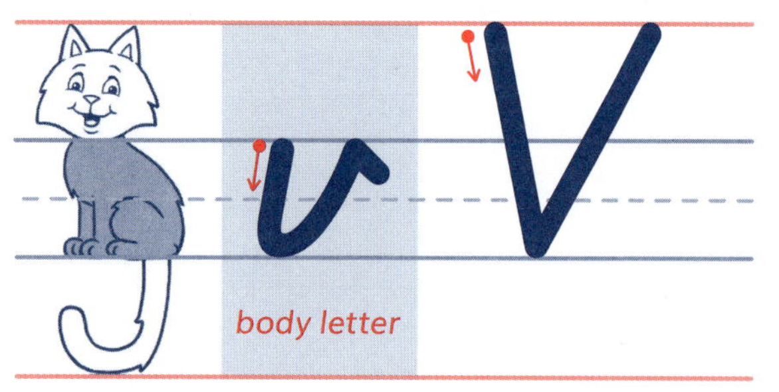

vase

Start at the red dot. Follow the arrow.

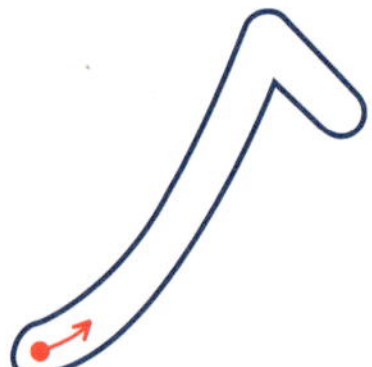 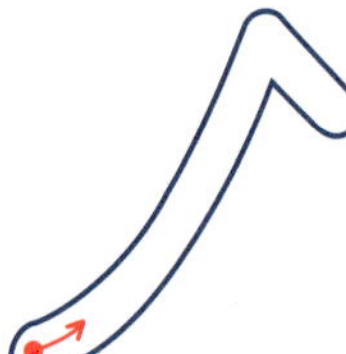 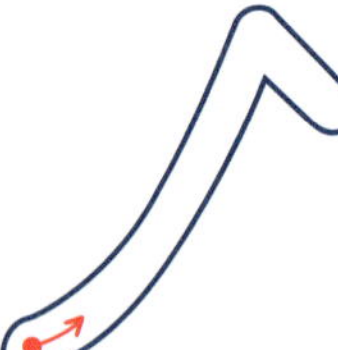 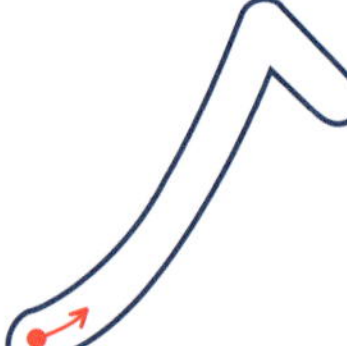 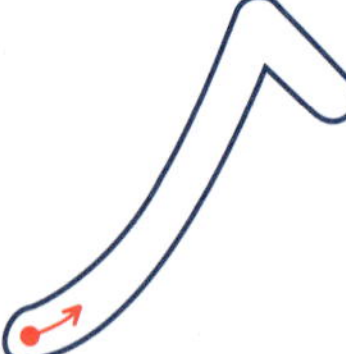

Track.

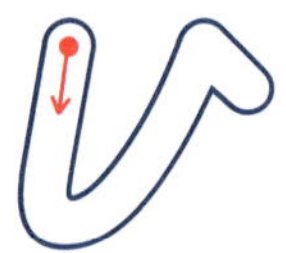 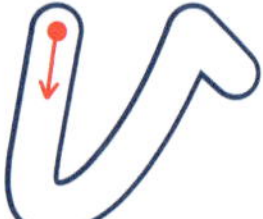  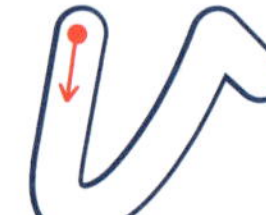 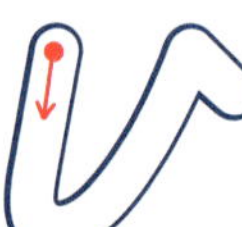

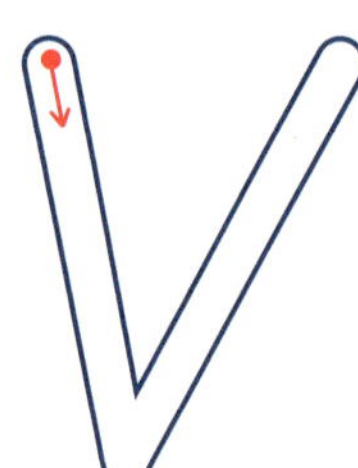 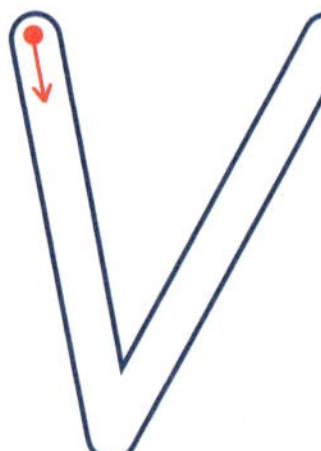 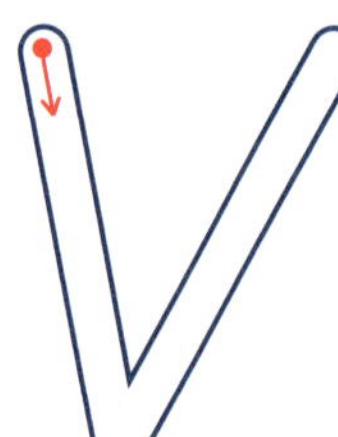 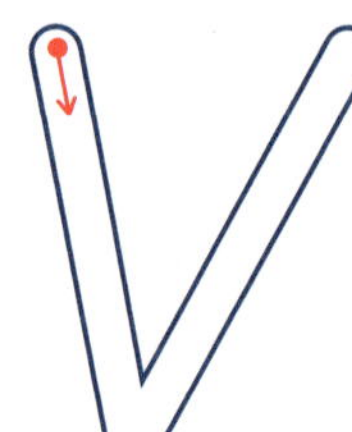 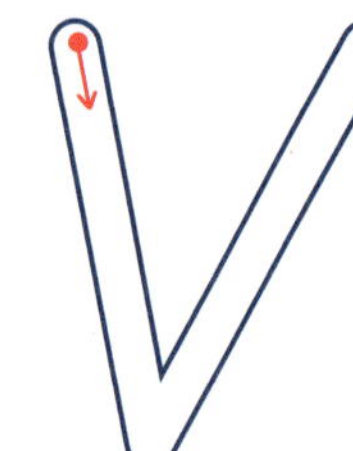

Find **v**.

  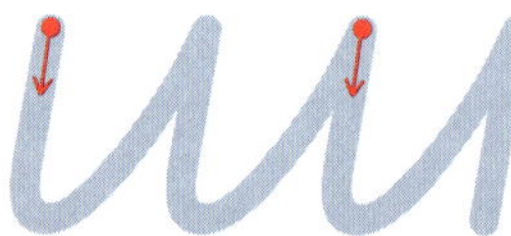

Trace and copy.

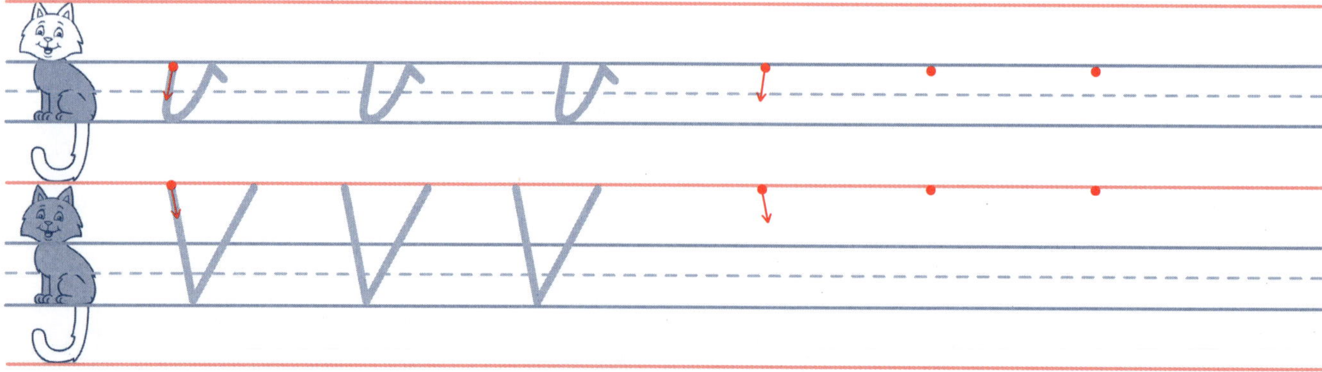

Trace and copy.

very very very

Trace and copy.

The bus said,

"I am very wet."

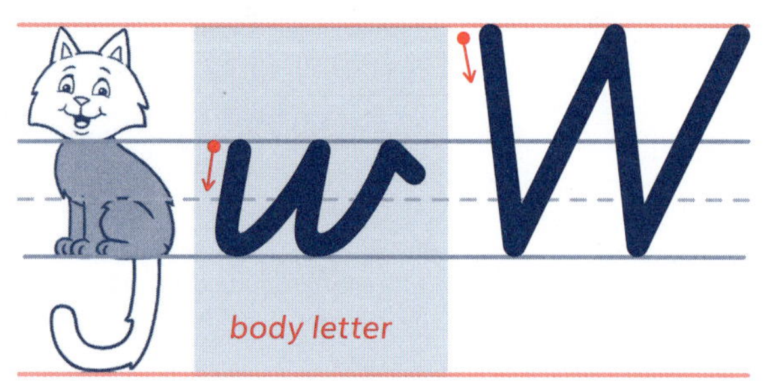

web

Start at the red dot. Follow the arrow.

Track.

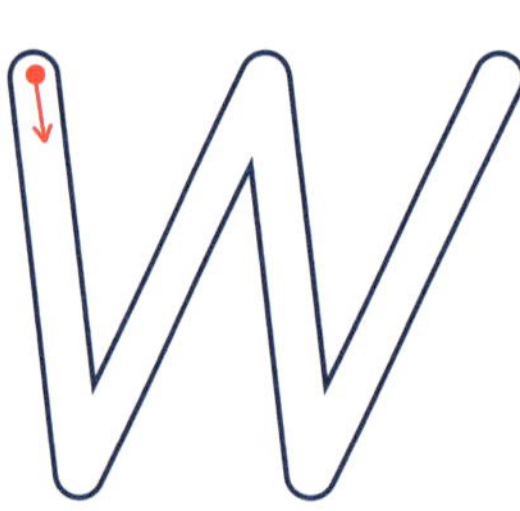

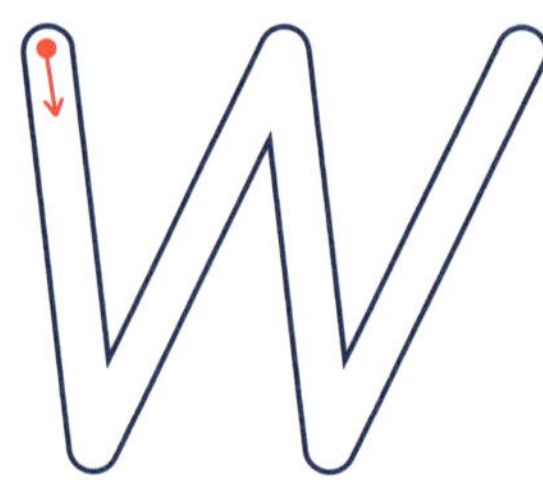

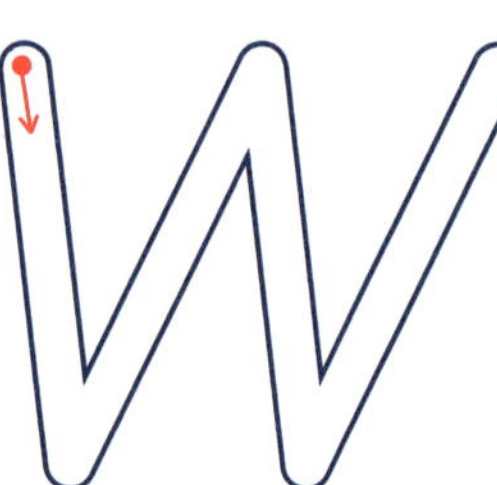

Find **w** and colour the wedge.

Trace and copy.

Trace and copy.

will will will will

Trace and copy.

"I will stop here

for a little rest."

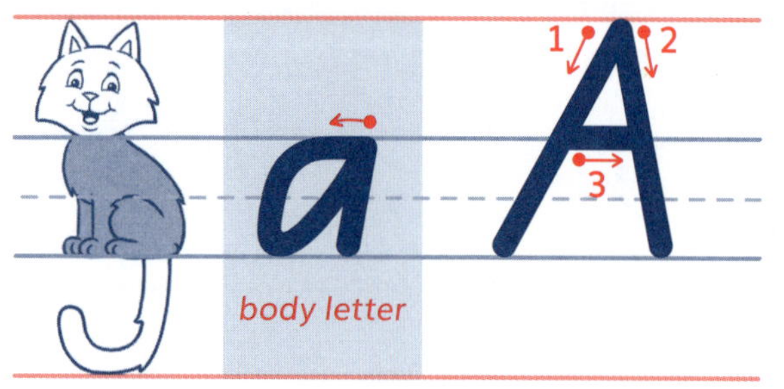

arm

Start at the red dot. Follow the arrow.

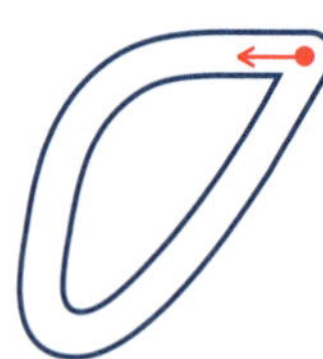 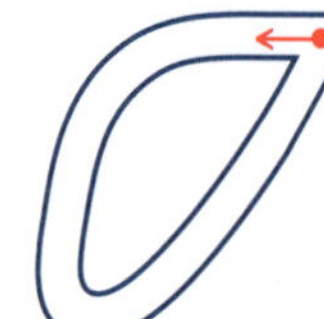 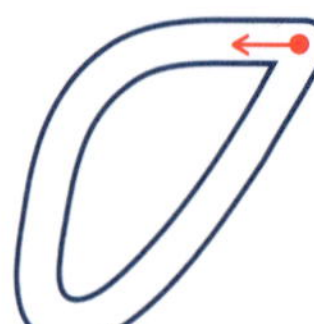 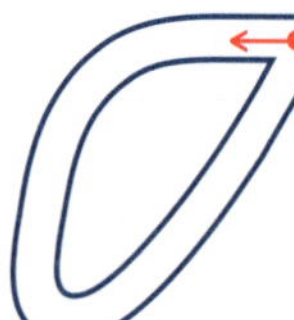 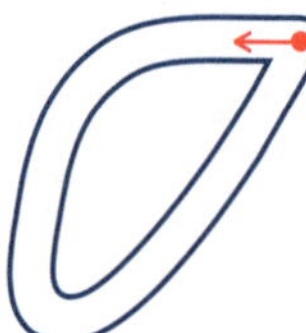

Track.

    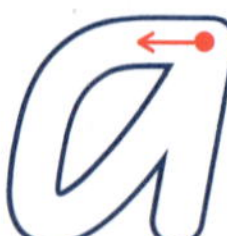

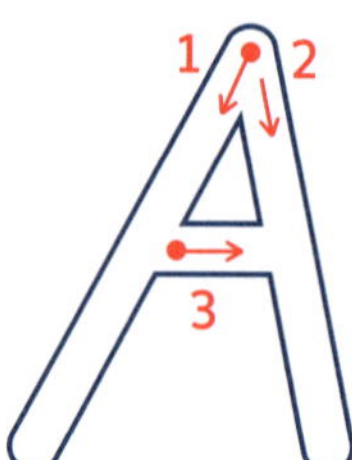

Find **a** and colour the wedge.

Trace and copy.

Trace and copy.

asleep asleep asleep

Trace and copy.

Soon, the Toytown

bus was fast asleep.

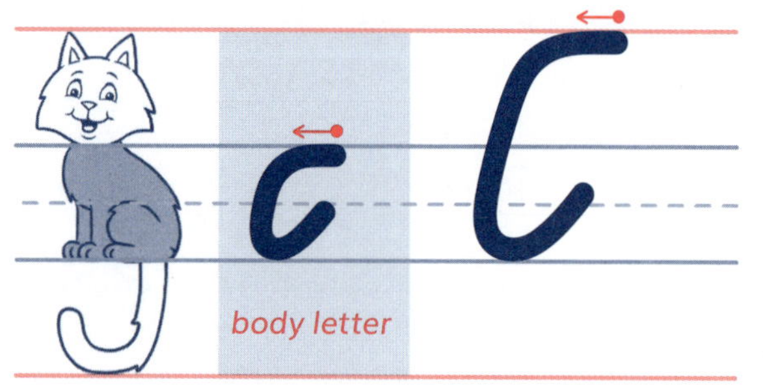

Start at the red dot. Follow the arrow.

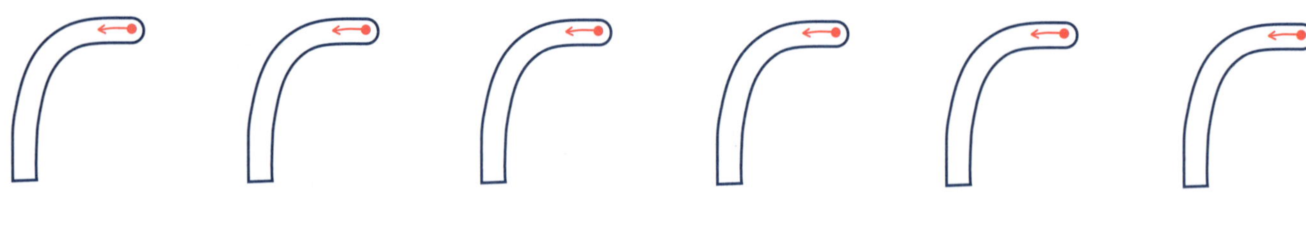

Track.

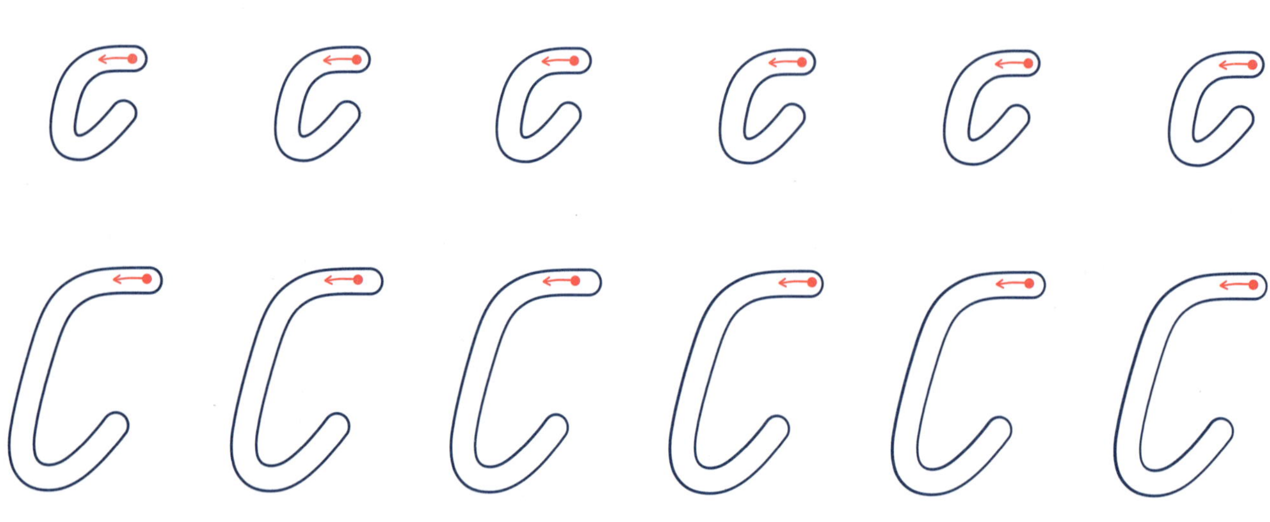

Find **c**.

Trace and copy.

Trace and copy.

came came came

get.ga/PMWA11

Trace and copy.

Toytown racing car

came down the hill.

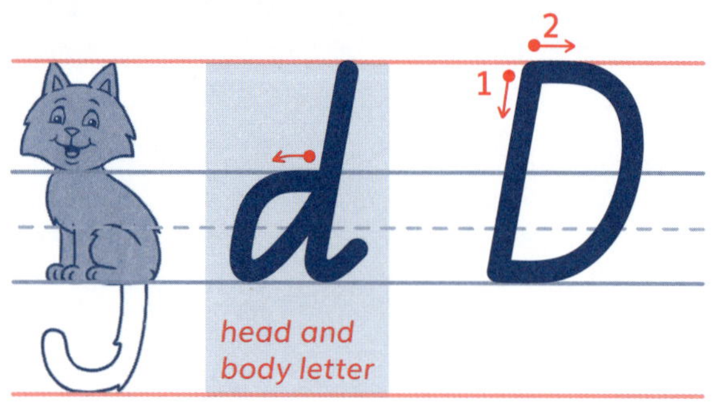

duck

Start at the red dot. Follow the arrow.

Track.

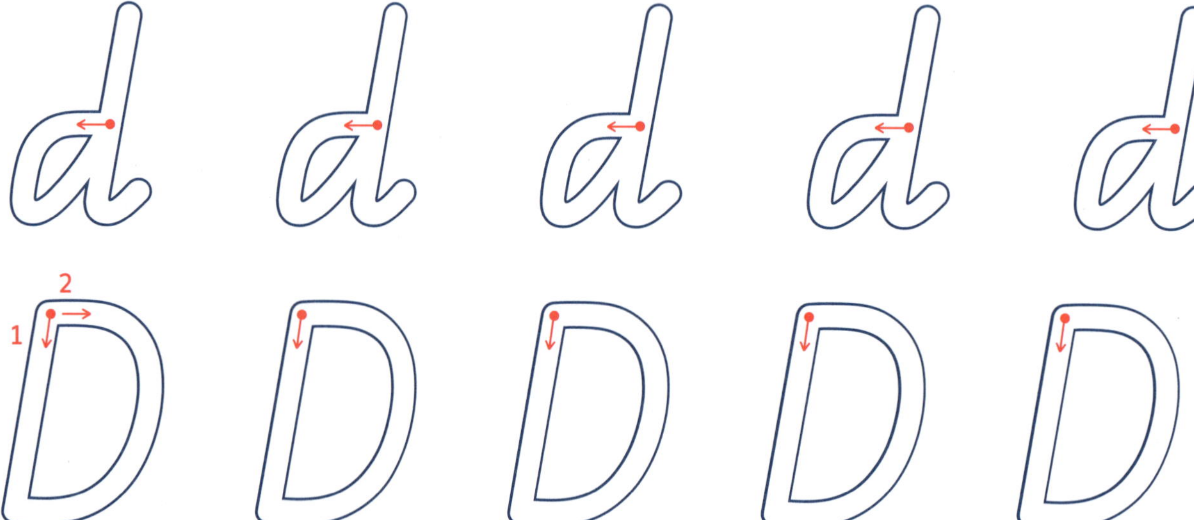

Find **d** and colour the wedge.

Trace and copy.

Trace and copy.

down down down

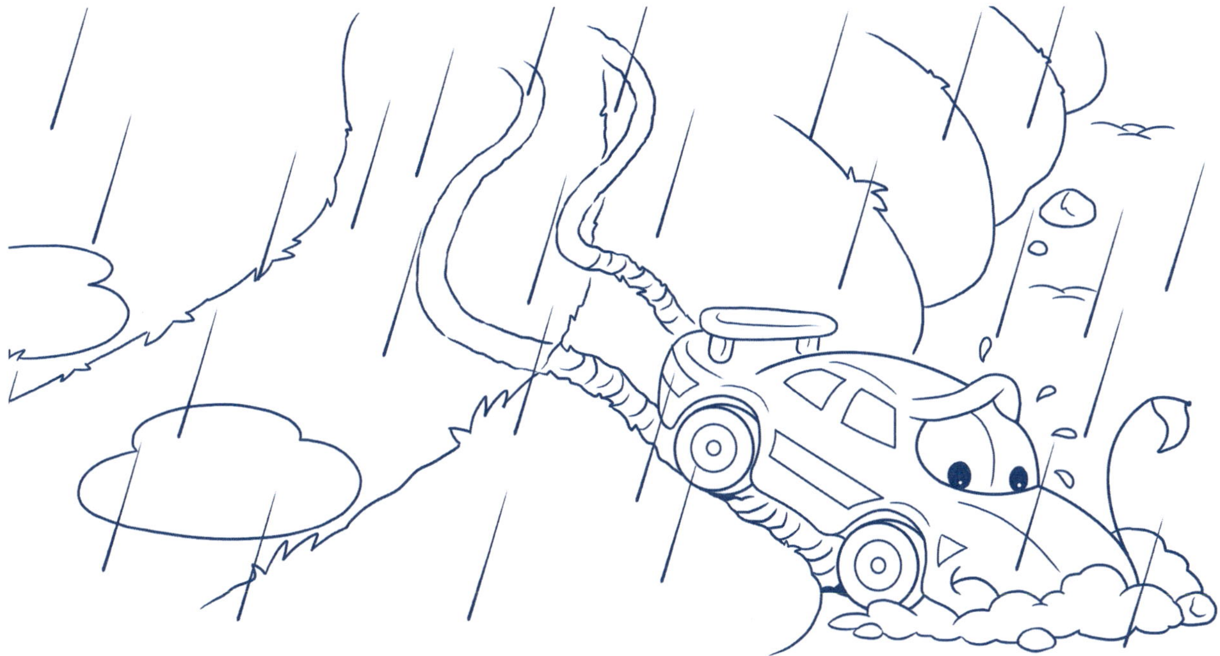

Trace and copy.

The racing car

was down in a ditch.

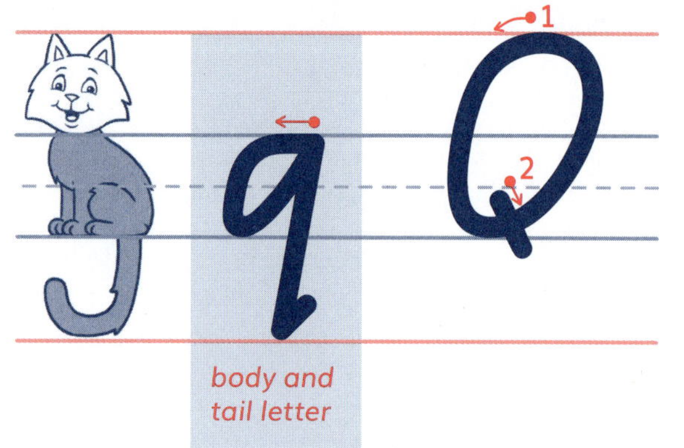

Start at the red dot. Follow the arrow.

 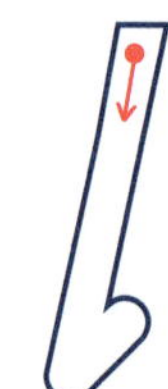 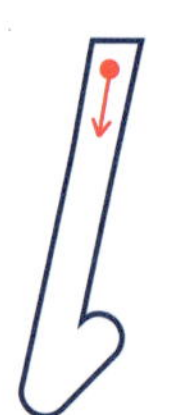  

Track.

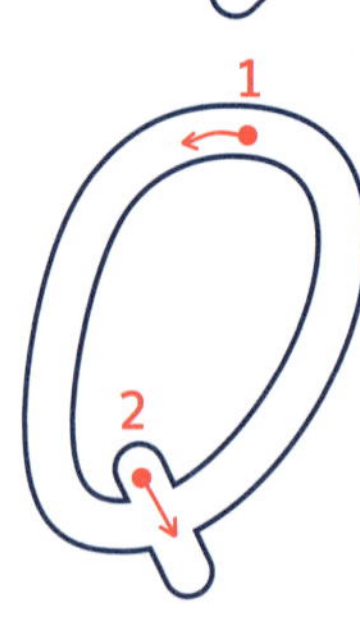

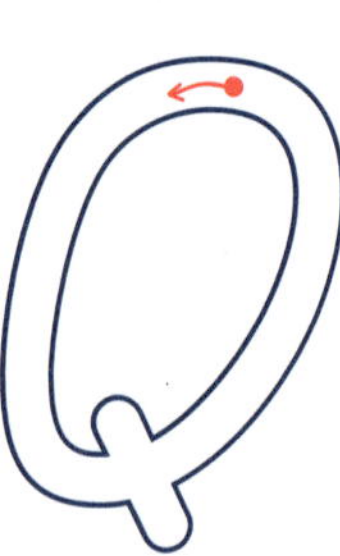 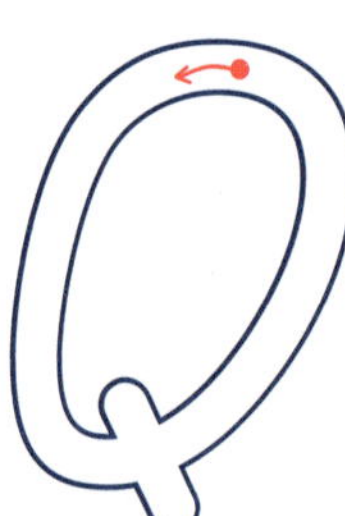 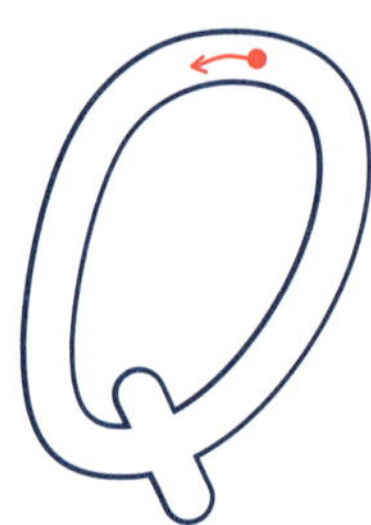 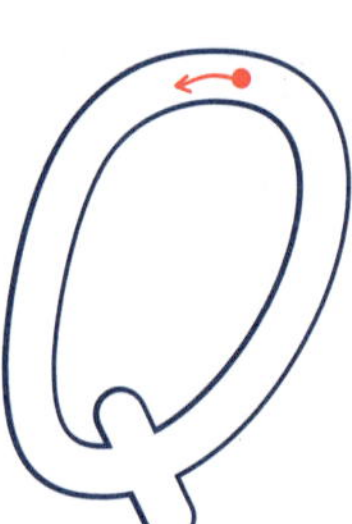

Find **q** and colour the wedge.

  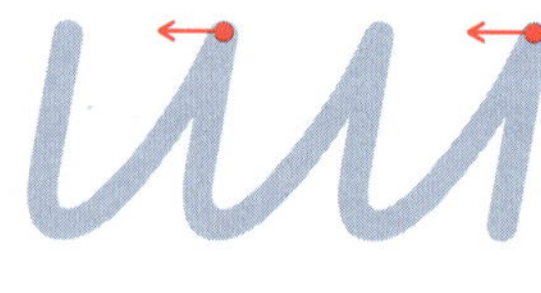

Trace and copy.

Trace and copy.

quickly quickly quickly

Trace and copy.

"Come quickly, tow truck. We need help!"

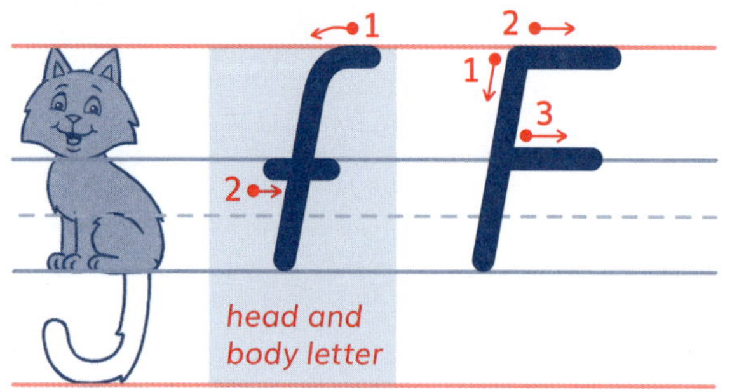

fish

Start at the red dot. Follow the arrow.

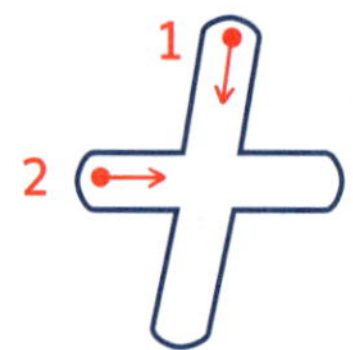
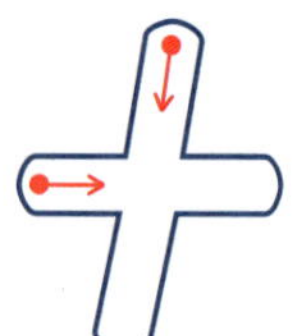
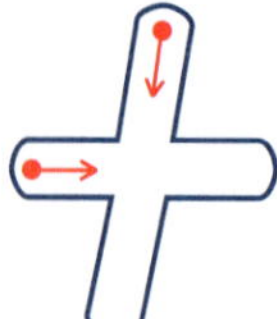
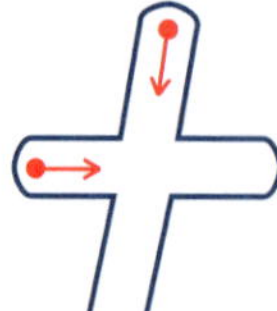
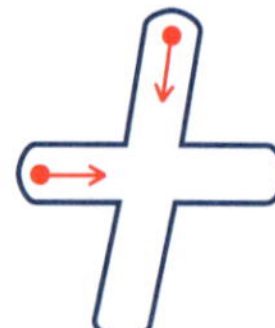

Track.

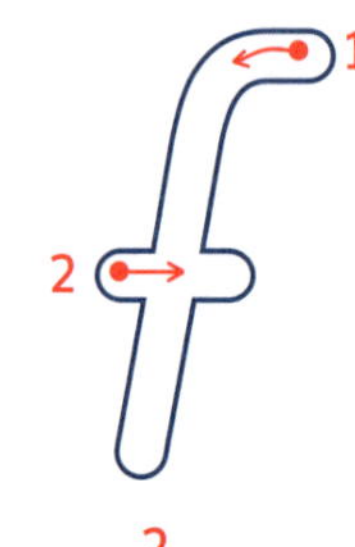

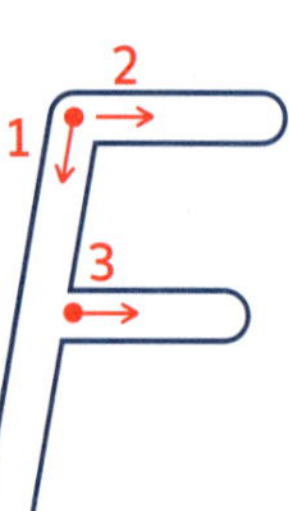

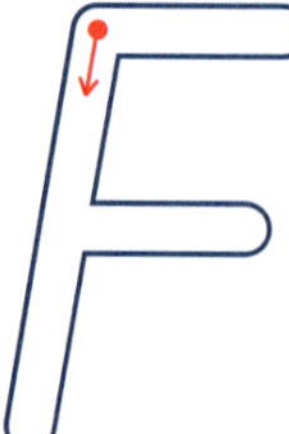
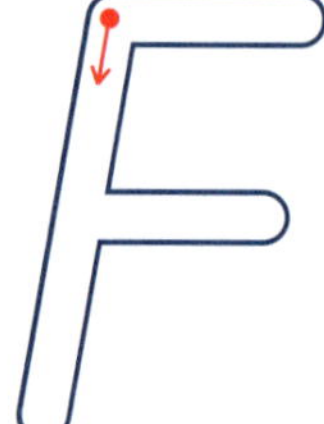

Find **f**.

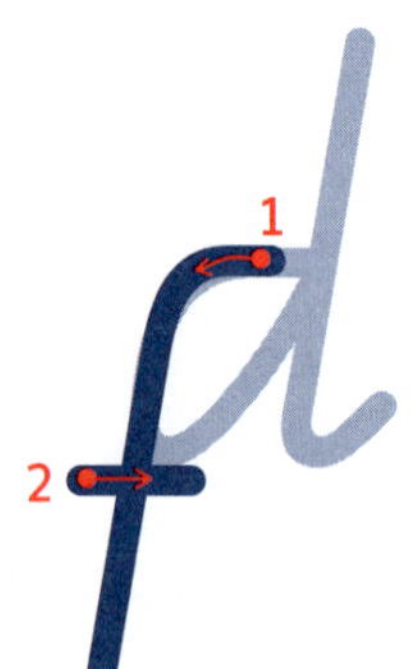

Trace and copy.

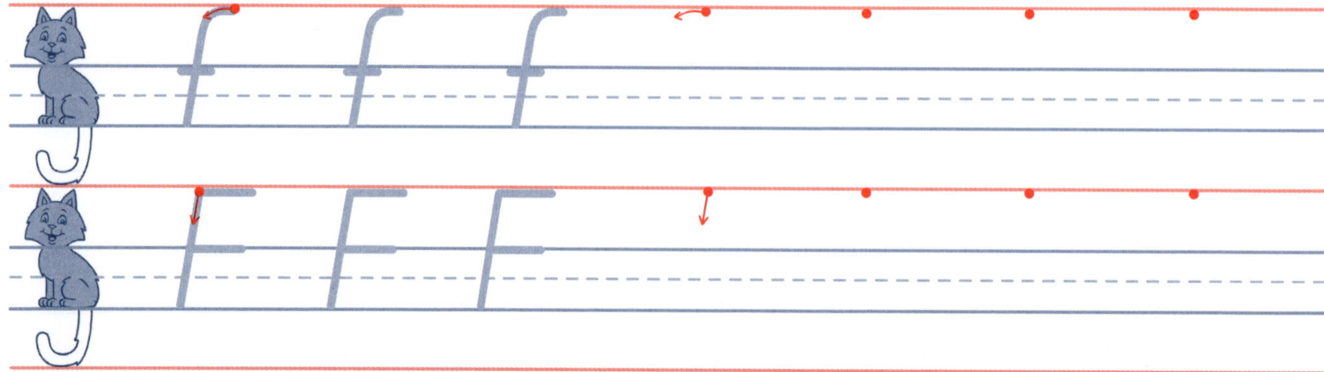

Trace and copy.

Trace and copy.

Toytown racing car

felt very scared.

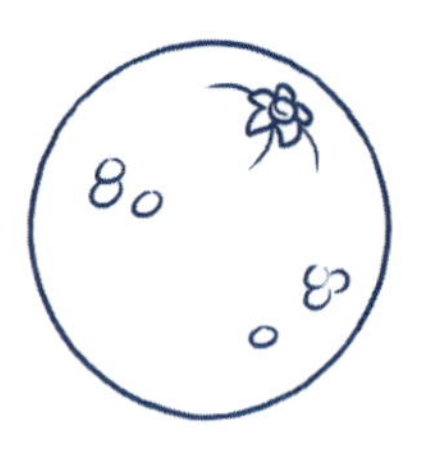

orange

Start at the red dot. Follow the arrow.

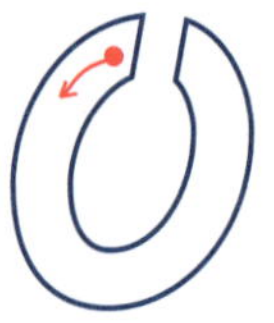 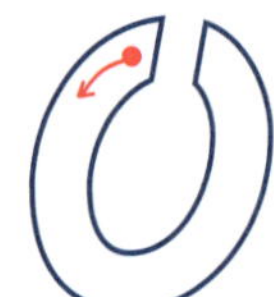 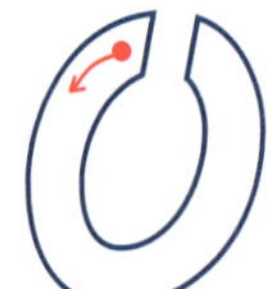   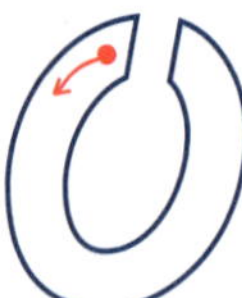

Track.

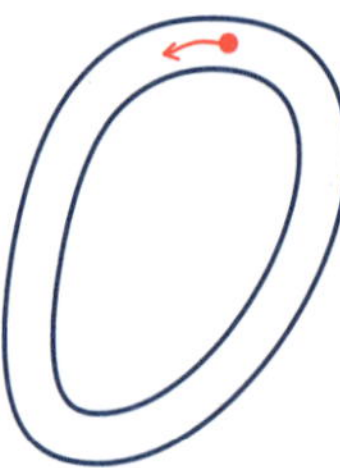 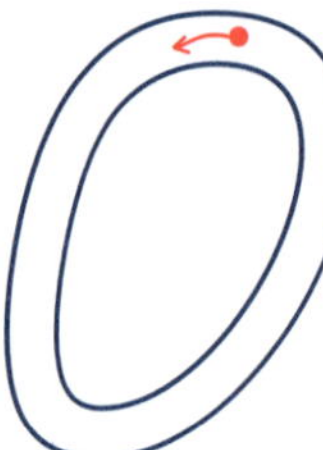 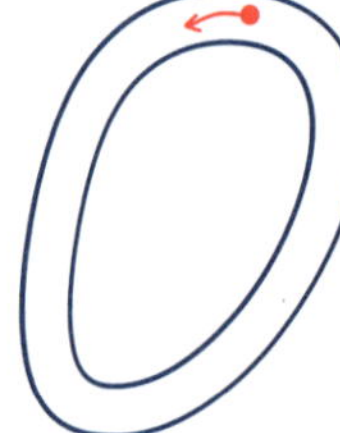 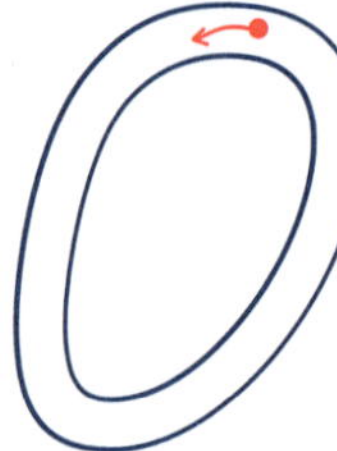 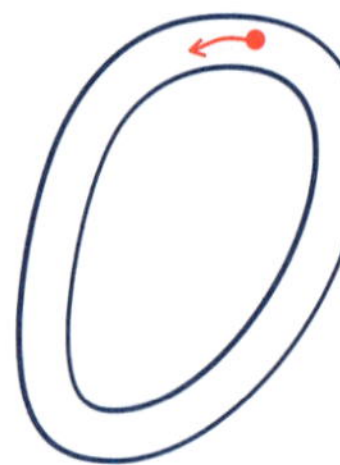

Find **o**.

Trace and copy.

Trace and copy.

out out out out

Trace and copy.

Tow truck pulled

the racing car out.

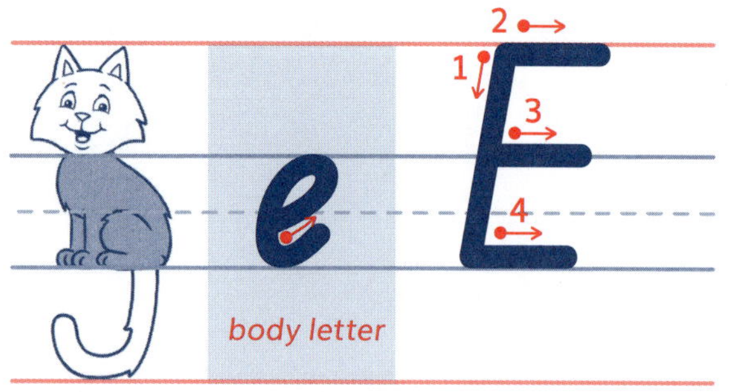

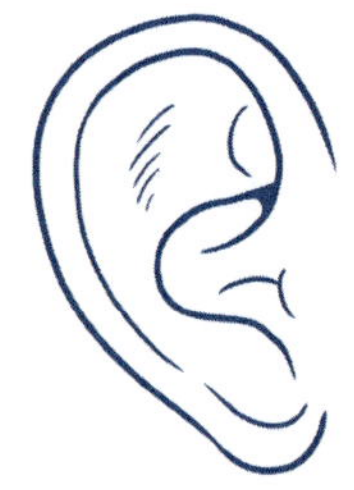

ear

Start at the red dot. Follow the arrow.

Track.

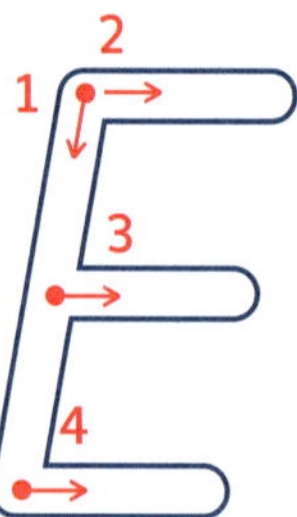

Find **e**.

Trace and copy.

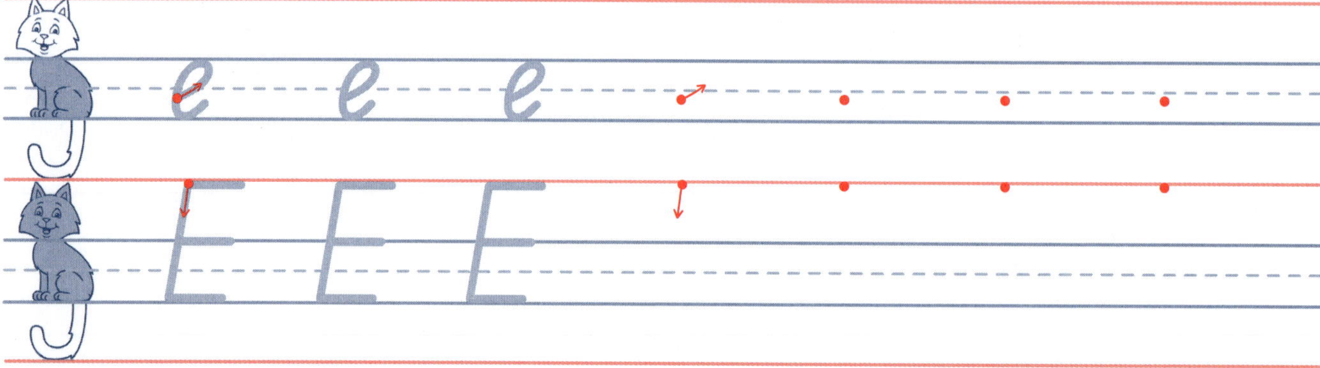

Trace and copy.

end end end end

get.ga/PMWA12

Trace and copy.

Everyone was happy

in the end.

Start at the red dot. Follow the arrow.

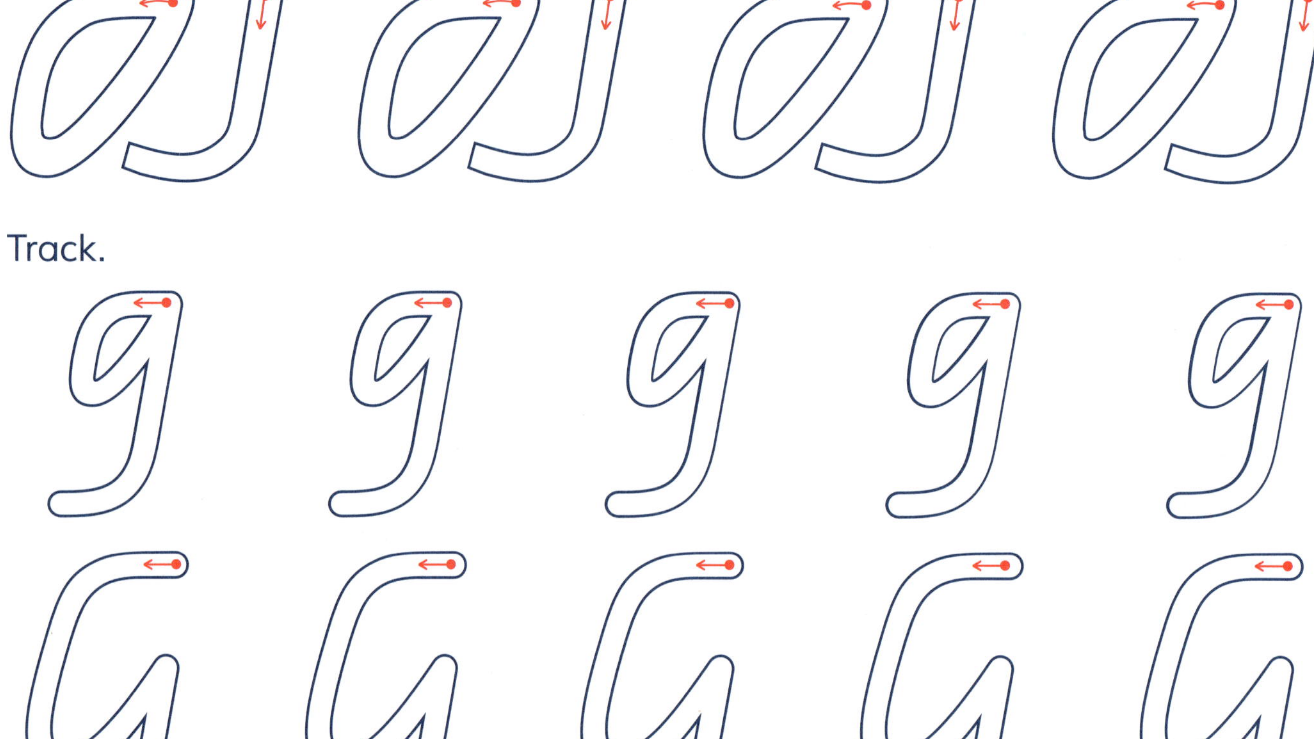

Track.

Find **g** and colour the wedge.

Trace and copy.

Trace and copy.

going going going

Trace and copy.

Racing car was going

around the bend.

yawn

Start at the red dot. Follow the arrow.

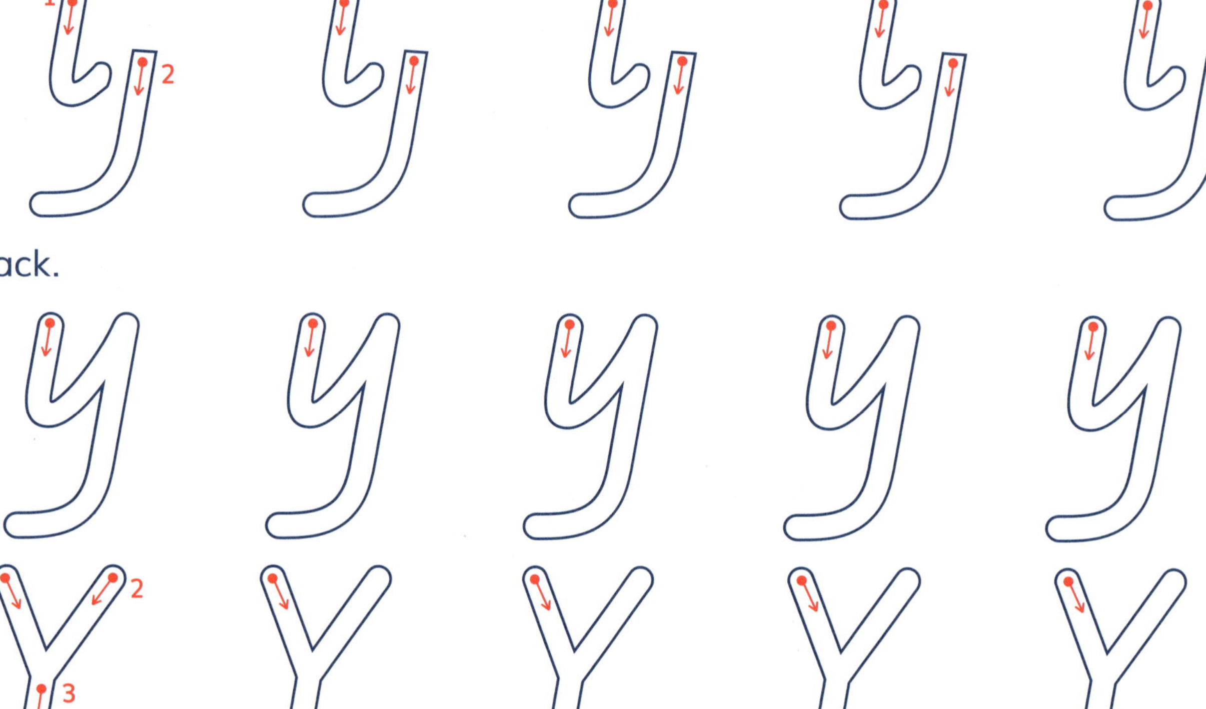

Track.

Find **y** and colour the wedge.

Trace and copy.

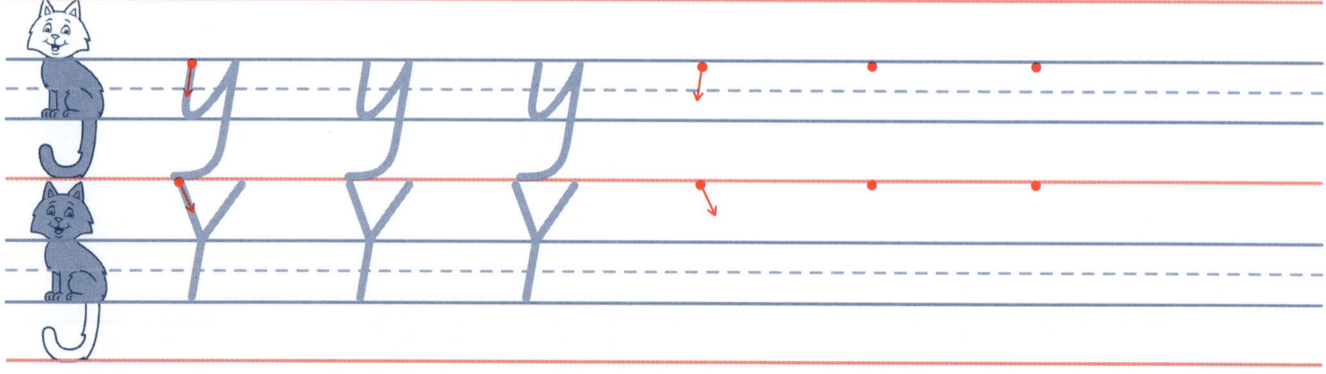

Trace and copy.

your your your your

Trace and copy.

"Driving fast might

hurt your friends!"

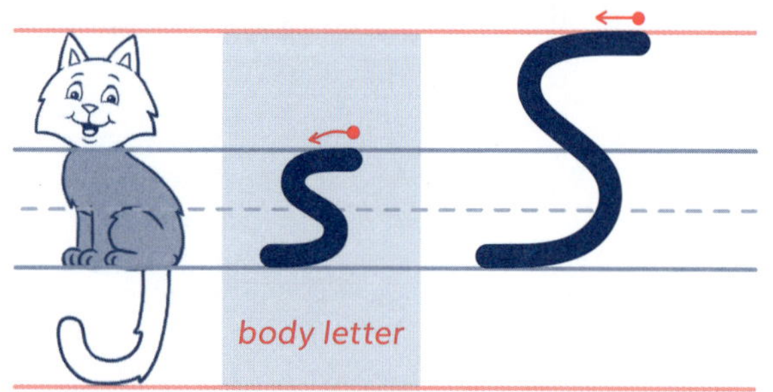

shoe

Start at the red dot. Follow the arrow.

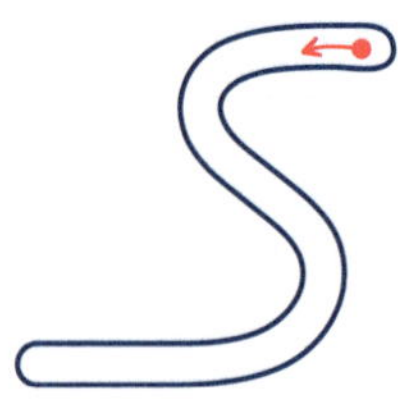 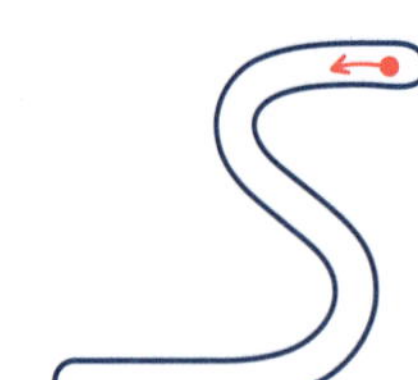 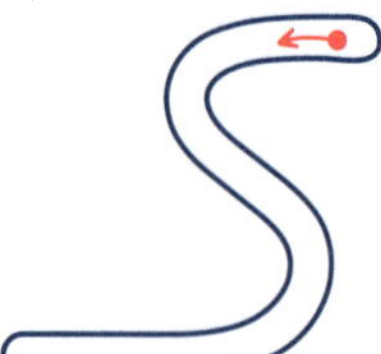 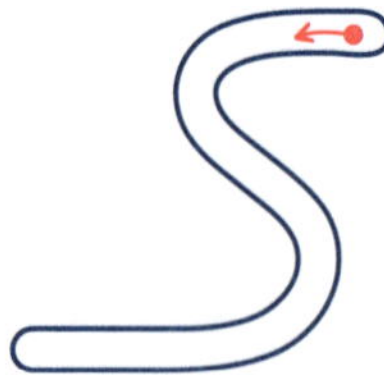

Track.

Find **s**.

 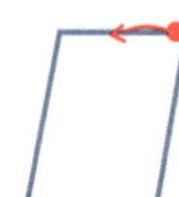 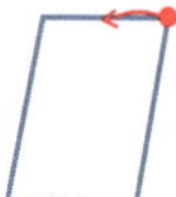 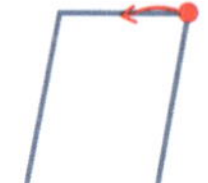 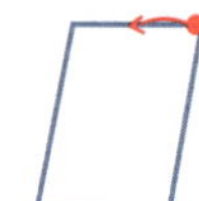 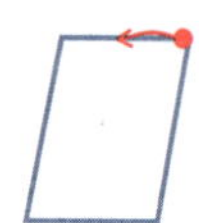

Trace and copy.

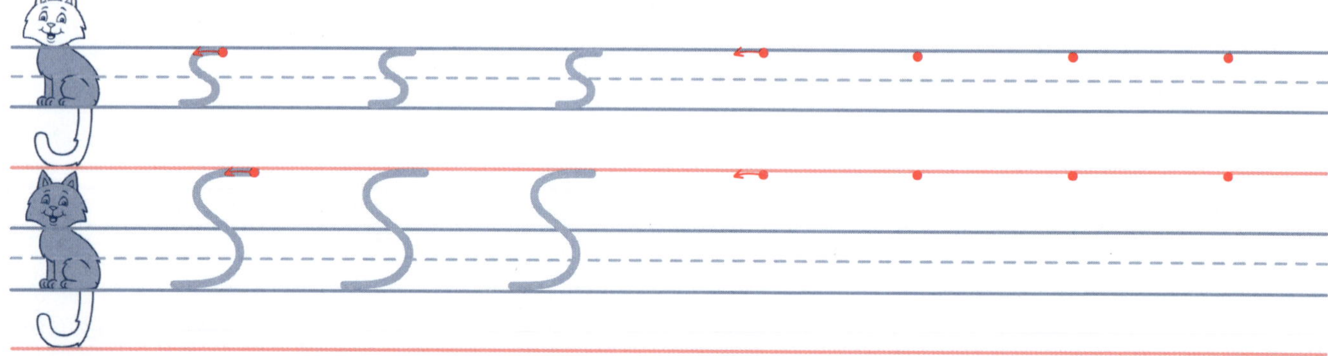

Trace and copy.

said said said said

get.ga/PMWA13

Trace and copy.

The police car said,

"This must end!"

Trace and copy.

1 one

2 two

3 three

4 four

5 five

6 six

7 seven

8 eight

9 nine

10 ten

Trace and copy.

20 twenty

30 thirty

40 forty

50 fifty

60 sixty

70 seventy

80 eighty

90 ninety

100 one hundred

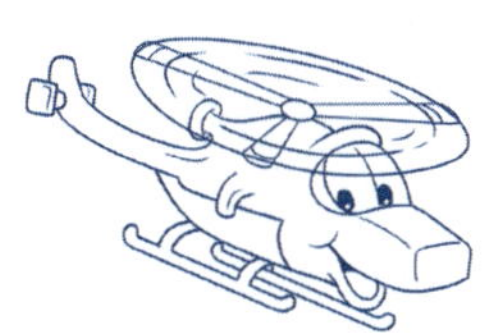

get.ga/PMWA14

Teacher observation guide

Student is: left-handed ☐ right-handed ☐

Student demonstrates correct posture, paper position and pencil grip. ☐

Student is stroking from top to bottom. ☐

Student is stroking from left to right. ☐

Student is tracking accurately. ☐

Student is tracing accurately. ☐

Student follows simple verbal rehearsal to form letters. ☐

Student forms lower-case letters with accuracy:

a	b	c	d	e	f	g	h	i	j	k	l	m	n	o	p	q	r	s	t	u	v	w	x	y	z

Student forms capital letters with accuracy:

A	B	C	D	E	F	G	H	I	J	K	L	M	N	O	P	Q	R	S	T	U	V	W	X	Y	Z

Student can write the numerals 1–100. ☐

Student uses head, body and tail character to describe the spatial properties of letters. ☐

Student can identify wedges within a letter pattern. ☐

Student is placing letters correctly within lines. ☐

Student can copy a word with accuracy. ☐

Student can copy a complete sentence with accuracy. ☐

Notes:

....

....

Date: ....

CERTIFICATE

get.ga/PMWC2